Luscious
COCONUT
DESSERTS

by LORI LONGBOTHAM

Photographs by LUCY SCHAEFFER

CHRONICLE BOOKS
SAN FRANCISCO

IF YOU ARE EVER SHIPWRECKED, HOPE FOR AN ISLAND WITH COCONUTS.

FOR JUDITH SUTTON, WITH GRATITUDE. I COULDN'T DO IT WITHOUT YOU.

ACKNOWLEDGMENTS:

Many thanks to Bill LeBlond and Amy Treadwell. And to Jerry Goldman; Auntie Jean; Steve, Liz, and Sarah; Ellen McGill; Catherine Longbotham; and the Perrys.

My thanks for good cheer and solace from Deborah Mintcheff; Barbara Ottenhoff; Barbara Howe; Jean Pellegrino; Beth Galton; Carol Prager; Marie Regusis; Joanna and Leigh; Sabra Turnbull; Lisa Troland; Rosie and Sprocket; Val Cipollone; Tracey Seaman; Jim Standard; Diana Sturgis; Sarah Mahoney; Kate Reese; Kathy Blake; Miriam Brickman; Kristine Kidd; Beth Lipton; Denise Mickelsen; Rebecca Freedman; Jena Myers and her parents, Jon and Debby; and Eugenia Escobar.

Library of Congress Cataloging-in-Publication Data available.

ISBN 978-0-8118-6599-9

Manufactured in China.

Designed by Andrew Schapiro
Prop styling by Dani Fisher
Food styling by Heidi Johannsen

The photographer wishes to thank Juliska, Match, mud australia,
Rose and Radish, Versace for Rosenthal, and William Yeoward Crystal.

10 9 8 7 6 5 4 3 2 1

Chronicle Books LLC
680 Second Street
San Francisco, California 94107
www.chroniclebooks.com

TABLE OF CONTENTS

INTRODUCTION

Unique, fascinating, and an enduring romantic symbol of the tropics, the coconut palm gives shelter in a storm and on sun-beaten beaches, and it provides a constant supply of food and drink. The tree is indispensable to the daily existence of millions who live in the tropics. In Sanskrit, it is called *kalpa vriksha*, "the tree that produces all the necessities of life." Coconuts are the staff of life and the secret of good health where they are grown and are a well-loved favorite almost everywhere else.

The coconut is the fruit and seed of the coconut palm, *Cocos nucifera*, meaning, loosely, "face-bearing nut," of the *Palmaceae* family. It is not a nut, although it is often categorized as one. It's a fibrous drupe, meaning a fruit with a hard stone (apricots and cherries are also drupes). A young coconut is very like a fruit, but a ripe coconut seems more like a nut. The meat is dense, oily, and found inside a very hard shell.

Coconut is enjoyed in two forms: the liquid and very soft flesh from young, or green, coconuts and the meat of the mature coconut. A large young coconut may contain up to a quart of refreshing drink. This liquid is not coconut milk, which is prepared by adding hot water to shredded mature coconut meat and then straining it. The jelly-like flesh of a young coconut is a great delicacy. It's called spoon coconut in Hawaii, because it is soft enough to be eaten with a spoon. As a coconut ripens, the coconut water is absorbed by the flesh, which hardens into coconut meat.

The coconut signifies tropical paradise, and I suggest that you bring that heaven right into your kitchen. *Luscious Coconut Desserts* has all of your old favorite recipes for coconut desserts, plus many fresh and exciting new ones. The coconut is one of a kind. It is a food and refreshment package, and it may be the only food that is naturally organic, since the meat is well protected from any pesticides. Coconut is a "love it madly" or an "I can totally do without it" thing, but there are many more of us coconut lovers than those who can live without it.

Coconut can stand alone beautifully in a dessert, but it also combines very well with other flavors, especially with tropical fruits—their flavors are beautifully complementary. Think coconut paired with pineapple, mango, banana, ginger, lychee, lemongrass, or dark chocolate. Coconut is excellent with all of those big flavors that shine brightly like the midday sun on a tranquil isle.

Coconut also marries strikingly with citrus fruits like mandarins, oranges, tangerines, limes, and clementines. Berries are also a treat with coconut, and the combination of raspberries, mango, and fresh coconut is one of my favorites. Stone fruits are another good companion, particularly apricots, nectarines, and cherries, as are nuts, especially tropical nuts such as Brazil nuts, macadamias, and cashews.

A list of favorite coconut desserts is truly an inventory of sweets from around the world. No matter where they are from, almost everyone has a coconut favorite from childhood.

Coconuts may speak to us of warm silky breezes, turquoise waters, and swaying palms, but they also speak of the lost Eden of childhood, even if you grew up in Cleveland.

Here you will find a very diverse compilation of recipes and flavor combinations from the American South, India, the Middle East, France, Italy, the Caribbean, North Africa, and England. You'll also be introduced to some unusual dishes, as well as unconventional uses for coconut, like Bananas Foster Shortcake with Coconut Biscuits (page 102), coconut biscuits topped with that classic banana dish. Another recipe you won't find in just any cookbook is the one for Elegant Coconut and Curry Butter Cookies (page 77), which takes the natural affinity between curry powder and coconut and turns it into a sweet, crumbly cookie.

I'm excited about all my fellow coconut lovers making these recipes. I have not only used products that are easy to find and to work with but that give great results. Just a few recipes call for a fresh coconut—more wouldn't be very practical, as preparing fresh coconut is a considerable amount of work. I think using fresh coconut makes the biggest difference when you're making a cake, and so that is where I have concentrated its use in this book.

ALL ABOUT COCONUT

THE TREE

When we live in cities at a fast pace, it is almost impossible not to get disconnected from the natural world. Food is one of the few things in our daily life that can help us strengthen that bond. Maybe we need to remind ourselves that coconut comes from a tree, not from little blue bags in the supermarket.

There are two main types of coconut palm, dwarf and tall, encompassing a large number of varieties. The dwarf variety produces more nuts than the tall palm but it has a shorter lifespan. The dwarf tree generally reaches twenty-five to thirty feet. The tall coconut palm commonly grows to eighty feet, although it can reach up to one hundred. It bears fruit after six to twelve years and yields fifty to sixty coconuts annually.

The principal growing regions for coconut are within twenty-two degrees north and south of the equator. Coconut palms like temperatures that never fall below 68°F, and they love rain. The trees grow primarily in salty, sandy soil near the sea.

The coconut palm is the most widely grown of all palm trees; it is found in more than eighty countries. The top coconut producers are the Philippines, Indonesia, Thailand, Central America, and Africa. The United States and Europe are the leaders in importing coconut products; combined, they account for about 55 percent of coconut exports.

THE FRUIT

A young coconut and a ripe coconut are two very different food products.

⁘ YOUNG COCONUT

Young coconuts have bright green husks and white interiors. They contain their maximum liquid of about four cups at around four months. At that point, the meat begins to form inside the shell as a thin, white, jelly-like layer. Ten years ago, young coconuts were almost impossible to find in the United States. Now they are sold in specialty produce markets and some supermarkets, and their liquid, packed in aseptic boxes, cans, or bottles, can be found in supermarkets, delis, and specialty and health food stores.

The sweet, fragrant juice of a young coconut is clear, almost opalescent, and as thin as water, with a subtle floral fragrance. It is the most cooling beverage I know; I recommend drinking it chilled. It is fat free and cholesterol free, and it's an excellent source of potassium, calcium, magnesium, phosphorous, and sodium. It is touted as an electrolyte-replacing beverage, better than any sports drink. It is said to enhance vitality, ease digestion, and even cure hangovers. Fresh young coconut water has a shelf life of about 2 weeks if refrigerated. The thin layer of young coconut flesh can be added to fruit salads or eaten right out of the shell, my favorite way.

Buy young coconuts husked and already opened. They are difficult to open at home—the woody green shell is thick and needs to be hacked off in one motion with something very sharp and heavy. Take the coconut home, and you can insert a straw and drink the liquid, then use a spoon to eat the soft flesh.

If you're buying packaged young coconut water, make sure it is 100 percent pure—with no preservatives, sugar, or other additives. I've been the happiest with packaged coconut water from the United States, Brazil, and Thailand; Vita Coco brand from Brazil is my current favorite.

⁞• MATURE (RIPE) COCONUT

The brown hard-shelled coconuts we buy in markets look nothing like what grows on the beautiful palms. Coconuts grow in bunches of eight to twelve and develop between the vertical leaves at the crown of the palm. Ripe coconuts can be either elongated or round and from four to six inches long. The coconuts hanging on the tree have a smooth outer covering, the husk. Inside is a thick layer of coarse brown fibers, covering the shell and fruit.

As young coconuts mature, the liquid inside hardens into coconut flesh, or meat, at about seven months, with full maturity at one year, when almost all the liquid has solidified. If not harvested earlier, the ripe fruits will fall from the tree at about fourteen months, or slightly sooner if a strong wind brings down the harvest. A whole ripe coconut, as we see it in the market, is only the kernel of the fruit, in a brown shell, the husk having been removed before shipping. There are three dark indentations, also known as "eyes," at the stalk end. Two of these are only shallow dents, but the third has an opening through which the seed can find its way to the outside to put down roots if the coconut is left to germinate.

The shell contains the white, oily, fibrous flesh. Just under the shell is a thin brown coat called the peel. It covers the kernel, which contains the meat and has a hollow center. A fresh mature coconut usually weighs between 1½ and 2 pounds.

Choosing a Mature Coconut

When shopping for a coconut, pick a place that has a brisk turnover in coconuts, as it will be most likely to have high-quality fruit. Check out the whole batch of coconuts available in the market, and if some are not in good shape, try another store.

When you shake the coconut, you should feel lots of liquid sloshing around inside; a robust splashing sound is a great sign. If you don't feel liquid inside, there's probably a crack in the shell, and the juice leaked out. Coconuts can easily crack during shipping (imagine those hard shells banging together). A coconut should feel heavy for its size, an indication that it has lots of meat. The "eyes" are subject to mold, so check them to make sure they aren't moldy or moist; if mold gets inside the coconut, the rich meat will spoil quickly. Smell the eyes too; there should be no indication of fermentation.

Even if you follow all the directions for buying a fresh coconut, you can still get a dud. Consider buying an extra (or two), just in case you are disappointed in the first one. A bad coconut can ruin your plans.

If you buy a coconut wrapped in plastic or cellophane, unwrap it after taking it home, to help prevent mold. In the best circumstances, fresh ripe coconuts will keep at cool room temperature for up to 2 weeks or in the refrigerator for up to 1 month. Once opened, they must be wrapped tightly and stored in the refrigerator, where they will last for about a week at most. You can freeze the flesh for up to 3 months.

Preparing a Mature Coconut

Opening a mature coconut can be daunting. Trying to pierce the eyes can be dangerous. There isn't really a lot of liquid in a ripe coconut anyway, and you don't really have to save it—it's not why you want the coconut.

When I was a child and we were lucky enough to have an occasional fresh coconut, we just walked outside and threw the coconut as hard as we could onto the patio or driveway. It worked, and you can do it that way too, but there are better choices.

Some coconuts are sold scored around their equator to make cracking easier—and that is a wonderful thing. Look for them in your local market or order them online. (Try www.melissas.com; they also offer young coconuts.)

Probably the method with the widest appeal is to wrap the coconut in a kitchen towel, place it on the floor or ground, or in the sink, and smack it with a hammer until it cracks open. The towel will keep pieces of the shell from flying around (don't use your favorite towel, as the hammer can tear it).

My favorite way to open a mature coconut is something I learned from Kasma Loha-unchit, a Thai food and culture expert. It works beautifully: Pick up the coconut with your left hand (if you are right-handed), with the middle of the coconut in the middle of your palm, and hold it over the sink or a bowl, and using the back, **not the sharp side**, of a heavy knife or cleaver, hit the coconut a few times all around the center, turning the coconut in your hand, until it cracks open cleanly. It will crack along a natural seam, separating into two nearly equal halves. You can do the same thing by holding the coconut in your hand and tapping it with a hammer all around the middle.

If you don't like the idea of hitting a coconut you are holding in one hand with a knife, there are other methods to try. Put the coconut on a baking sheet in a 325°F oven for about 20 minutes or so. The coconut shell will develop "fault lines," and the heat will loosen the meat from the shell; the coconut may even crack in the oven, which is fine. Just don't leave the coconut in the oven any longer than you have to—you don't want the meat to cook. Remove it from the oven and, when it is cool enough to handle, hit it along the fault lines with a hammer, heavy mallet, or the back of a knife or cleaver to crack it open.

Another alternative is to put the coconut in your freezer for an hour or two, then crack open the brittle frozen shell with a hammer. Or do as they do in Sri Lanka: Soak the coconut in hot water for 30 to 50 minutes, then hit it with a hammer, rotating the coconut until the shell cracks open into two halves.

After opening it, inspect and taste the coconut. It should have a subtle oily aroma and a nutty flavor. Its aroma should be fresh and sweet, with no moldy smell. Save or discard the liquid as you desire; if it tastes clean and sweet, you can use it to make coconut milk. Sometimes the water can be a little sour but the coconut flesh is just fine. Now you need to remove the white meat from the hard brown shell using a screwdriver, a table knife, or another sturdy tool such as an oyster knife. Insert the tool between the flesh and the shell, which will release something like a vacuum seal, and the coconut will pop away from the shell. If the piece of coconut is big, you may need to slip the screwdriver between the shell and the coconut in several different places around the edge to release the shell.

Peel the brown skin from the white flesh with a vegetable peeler, if desired. If making coconut ribbons, you may want to leave the peel on; it gives them a great look. Use a sharp peeler that doesn't remove any of the white flesh with the brown peel. Then rinse and dry the coconut meat.

Now you can shred or slice the coconut. You can shred it on the biggest holes of a box grater, but I prefer to use the food processor. Cut it into chunks and use the fine, medium, or large shredding blade of the processor. I cut the coconut into ½- to ¾-inch pieces and add it through the feed tube with the motor running.

To make fresh coconut ribbons, square off one of the edges of a large piece of coconut with a knife. Then use a vegetable peeler to cut strips the width of the coconut's thickness and as long as possible, or the size you choose. There are fantastic coconut shredders in Southeast Asia and South Asia. Some are small wooden stools in the shape of animals that you sit on while using the sharp ninja-star-like blade—be careful with those, they are very sharp. The same type of blade is also attached to a wooden paddle, which you set on a chair and hold down with your foot while shredding the coconut.

❧ TOASTING COCONUT

Use a large heavy baking sheet for toasting dried coconut. Preheat your oven to 350°F, and toast the coconut for 6 to 8 minutes. The coconut usually toasts around the edges first; as it toasts, just stir the toasted coconut into the center

and the still-white coconut to the outside with a wide metal spatula for even browning. Watching carefully is the most important thing. You probably will not need to stir the coconut until about halfway through, but if you stir it near the halfway mark and then again toward the end, you will end up with evenly toasted golden brown coconut. I prefer a deep golden brown to a paler one. After toasting a couple of batches, you will notice if your oven has a hot spot or two, and you can adjust accordingly—turning the pan around halfway through if necessary.

You also want to toast ribbons of fresh coconut at 350°F. Put about 1 cup coconut ribbons on a large heavy baking sheet and toast in the oven, stirring at least 3 times, for 18 to 20 minutes, until golden brown.

I prefer the taste of toasted coconut over raw in almost every case. It adds a depth of flavor and a warmth that is irresistible.

❧ FRESH COCONUT CREAM AND MILK

Coconut milk and cream are made by steeping shredded fresh coconut in boiling or hot water until the liquid is thick and creamy. Coconut milk has less protein than cow's milk and more fat. Like dairy milk, it is an emulsion, and if it is left to stand, the cream rises to the top. Coconut milk and cream are used in Asian desserts much in the same way that cow's milk and cream are used in the West.

Shred the coconut in the food processor with a fine or medium shredding blade before steeping it in hot water. I like a ratio of about 4 parts coconut to 3 parts water. So, if you have 2 cups of shredded coconut, use 1½ cups of boiling water. If you need more coconut milk, use 3 cups of coconut and 2¼ cups hot water. Cut the coconut into small pieces before you add it to the processor; I cut it into ½-inch cubes. Use the fine or medium shredding blade and add the coconut through the feed tube with the motor running. Then add the boiling or hot water through the feed tube and process until the mixture looks slushy. (I have a smaller food processor, so I add most of the water with the machine running and then, when it gets close to being full, turn off the machine and add the remaining water.) Transfer it to a bowl and let the mixture steep for about 25 minutes; when it is cool enough to handle, knead it with your hands to get as much coconut into the water as possible. After steeping, transfer the mixture to a clean kitchen towel or rinsed cheesecloth and twist it over a bowl to extract as much liquid as possible. From the 2 cups of coconut and the 1½ cups of water, you will get a generous 1½ cups coconut milk.

If you need coconut cream, pour the liquid into a glass measure and wait until the cream rises to the surface; it will separate faster in the refrigerator.

Some cooks use cow's milk instead of water to make coconut milk. I don't see any need for it; it has plenty of flavor without it. And coconut milk (both fresh and canned) offers an advantage over dairy—you can mix citrus juice or steep fresh ginger in it without it curdling.

Some books say you can make several batches of coconut milk from the same shredded coconut, steeping it twice or even three times. I recommend making only one batch per coconut.

Use fresh coconut milk immediately if possible, or the same day. Even if refrigerated, fresh coconut milk rarely keeps for 24 hours. It can turn sour quickly at room temperature, although a pinch of salt may slow the process. Some cooks bring it to a boil to extend its shelf life.

Making coconut milk using dried coconut is even easier. I also make this in the food processor. Finely grind 2 cups of shredded unsweetened dried coconut in the processor, transfer it to a bowl, and add 2 cups of boiling water. Let the mixture steep for about 35 minutes;

when it is cool enough to handle, knead it with your hands to get as much coconut into the water as possible. After steeping, transfer the mixture to a clean kitchen towel or rinsed cheesecloth and twist it over a bowl to extract as much liquid as possible. You should get a generous 1½ cups. (If you want more coconut milk, increase the quantities as desired, using equal parts of hot water and shredded coconut.)

❖ CANNED COCONUT MILK

You can buy first-rate, luscious coconut milk in cans these days; it is widely available in supermarkets and very handy. However, some brands are better than others (see my recommendations below). The coconut milk should be thick and rich and a pure, clean white. Some canned coconut milk captures the intense floral and fruity flavor of the tropics; in fact, a high-quality canned coconut milk can be better than what you could make at home. When made from the freshest, highest-quality coconuts, using heavy machinery to extract the coconut milk, it can be thicker and richer than any homemade version. It is difficult to find a canned coconut milk that is 100 percent pure; most brands contain an antioxidant such as citric acid and a preservative like sodium metabisulfite. Never buy canned coconut milk with added dextrins,

caseinates, or emulsifying agents like gums. Guar gum can prevent the coconut milk from separating into cream and milk and adversely affect the flavor and texture.

Try different brands and see which has the flavor and consistency you like best. My favorites are all from Thailand. My current preference is Chaokoh, which comes in a 13½-ounce can. Aroy-D (*aroy* means delicious in Thai) comes in both 14-ounce and 5.6-ounce cans, which are handy when you need only a small amount. Thai Kitchen has a 5½-ounce can as well as larger cans. I also like Mae Ploy brand, but it comes in a 19-ounce can, which is not as convenient as the others.

Canned organic coconut milk is available from Thailand, the Philippines, Indonesia, and the Dominican Republic. Again, I prefer the coconut milk from Thailand. Once opened, canned coconut milk should be refrigerated; it will keep for at least 2 days. Store it in a tightly covered container (not the can), and use it as soon as possible.

I think "lite" or "light" coconut milk is worthless. It is regular canned coconut milk with water added. We could do that ourselves—but why would we?

❖ CANNED COCONUT CREAM

Although I generally prefer scooping the thick cream from the top of a can of high-quality coconut milk, Aroy-D makes a canned coconut cream that is very thick; it comes in a 19-ounce can. There are several other brands too. Try a few and see what you think.

POWDERED COCONUT CREAM

Powdered coconut cream is prepared from mature coconuts at least one year old. I haven't found any that is 100 percent pure; even my favorite brand, Chao Thai, contains a type of sugar and preservatives. It comes in a foil package sealed inside a cardboard box and is available in two sizes, 5.6 ounces and 13 ounces. For a thick coconut cream, whisk together 3 tablespoons of the powder and 1 cup of warm water. For a thinner coconut cream, use 1 tablespoon of the powder and 1 cup warm water.

FROZEN COCONUT CREAM

Found in Asian markets, this is very rich, with an intense coconut flavor and a beautiful smooth texture. Thaw it in the refrigerator and use it quickly.

SHREDDED DRIED COCONUT

In my experience, two things most affect the flavor and texture of dried coconut: the size of the pieces and how dry the coconut is. The bigger the cut, the more flavor it will have. And you do not want the coconut to be totally dried out; a little remaining moisture makes a great difference, and the coconut will have more flavor. Dried coconut is available with a moisture content of up to 4 percent, so shop around and find a source for coconut that is not completely desiccated. If you select it carefully, it can have as much flavor as the very moist sweetened flaked supermarket coconut. I have had the best luck finding fine-quality unsweetened dried coconut in Asian and South Asian markets. Sometimes the larger-shred coconut is labeled "fancy shred" or "medium shred." Never buy shredded coconut that is yellow, not pure white; yellowing indicates that it is old.

There are many different sizes of shredded unsweetened dried coconut available, and, unfortunately, neither the sizes nor the names are standardized. Wide-cut is my favorite store-bought cut to toast and eat; I use it to make Candied Coconut (page 141) and as a garnish. Beautiful and graceful, these wide-cut strips are the closest you can get to fresh coconut. The wide-cut coconut I buy is 2 inches long and a generous ½ inch wide. If you can't find it in a shop near you, www.chefshop.com has it.

In the commercial dried coconut business, a "slice" is a generous ¼ inch wide and more than 1¼ inches long. If you can find

that size, and it is pure white (not yellow) grab it! Your best chance of finding it is at a very busy Asian market. The size called "chip" is the same width as "slice" but only ½ inch long. "Finely grated" coconut tends to be much smaller than coconut marked "shredded." "Tender flake" is about the same size as the sweetened flaked coconut available in the supermarket. "Special long thread" coconut is very thin and about 1 inch long; "extra fancy shred" is the same thickness and 2 to 3 inches long.

Commercial grated coconut is available in several different sizes: coarse, medium, macaroon, and extra fine, as well as a mix of all the sizes. These are all very small. Following the principle that the bigger the pieces, the more flavor the coconut will have, choose accordingly.

SWEETENED FLAKED COCONUT

Sweetened flaked coconut is dried coconut to which water and sugar have been added. Some say its flavor and mouthfeel are most similar to fresh coconut, but it is very sweet. The moisture level, which increases tenderness and enhances flavor, ranges from 10 to 15 percent. The sugar content is approximately 30 percent. Sweetened coconut generally has more flavor than unsweetened.

Store any type of dried coconut in an airtight container in a cool, dark place.

Because I am fond of toasted coconut, I often toast it before storing, and I think it helps it to keep longer. And when I decide to make a coconut dessert, I'm ahead—the coconut is already toasted. Untoasted dried coconut should keep for about 4 months at cool room temperature, 5 to 6 months in the refrigerator, and 8 to 12 months in the freezer.

CREAM OF COCONUT

Coco López is the most common brand of cream of coconut, a very sweet concoction that comes in 15-ounce cans. It is not suited for cooking or other desserts, in my opinion; I prefer to stick to ingredients that don't contain so much sugar. Sugar is the second ingredient listed on cans of cream of coconut, which is really a syrup; it also contains dozens of additives. Do not confuse this with coconut cream, which you can make with a fresh coconut and is also available powdered and as a liquid in cans.

FROZEN SHREDDED COCONUT

Frozen shredded coconut can be found in Asian and South Asian markets, in 14-ounce and 1-pound packages. It is perishable and does not last long after defrosting, so I usually thaw it in the refrigerator and plan on using it within a day. You can substitute it for fresh and other unsweetened coconut in some recipes.

❖ COCONUT AND PALM SUGAR

Although the names "palm sugar" and "coconut sugar" are sometimes used interchangeably, the sugars are not exactly the same. One comes from the sugar palm and the other from the coconut palm. They do both come from the sap that drips from cut flower buds.

You can find coconut and palm sugar in Asian markets or order it online. The sugar may be pale creamy beige or a dark caramel brown, and soft and gooey or rock hard, depending on how long the sap was reduced; and the color, consistency, and sweetness can vary from batch to batch and from country to country. You can use either sugar for the recipes in this book. That is a good thing, both because you won't always know which one you are buying (they are not always labeled) and because you will not always have a choice. If you find the sugar in a plastic jar and you can tell by pressing the jar that the sugar is soft, buy it—then you can just spoon it out. The soft, moist type is often sold in wide-mouth jars, which make it very easy to spoon out the sugar. However, the hard version keeps better. If the sugar is hard, you need to shave, crush, or grate it before you can measure it, and that is why I have indicated in the recipes to shave the sugar, but if you have a soft sugar, just fill the measuring spoon. It is easier to deal with hard sugar that is not in a jar; choose one in a cellophane package. The hard sugar is often molded in coconut shell halves. The hard and soft sugars are both available in cans, but I prefer to see what I'm buying. When I have a choice, I usually choose the darkest palm sugar, because it seems to have more flavor; some taste of a rich caramel. (Please be aware that unrefined cane sugar is also sold in these same forms—so pay attention.) Store palm sugar in a cool, dry place.

I once visited a family on central Java in Indonesia when the woman of the house happened to be making coconut palm sugar. It was a fascinating experience. The sap she'd gathered from the flowers was light colored and slightly cloudy. She built a roaring fire using coconut husks and fibers under a long, low terra-cotta stove; it was not even twelve inches tall. The sap went into wok-like pans, which she set over the fire and boiled down to a thick syrup. Then she beat it to a smooth, creamy texture with a paddle. She poured it into small coconut shell halves and left it to set and harden. It was delicious! Dark and rich, with a big flavor, it had a faint essence of coconut.

❖ COCONUT RUM

My preference is for Malibu rum, made in the tropical paradise of Canada. Bacardi and others also make coconut rum. Malibu comes in an opaque white bottle, but it is colorless, like light rum.

❧ COCONUT EXTRACT

I searched high and low for a good-quality pure coconut extract (there are many imitation flavorings out there, but it is not worth it to go to all the trouble to make a dessert and use a fake extract), and I have found a couple that I like quite a lot. I got them both at Kalustyan's in New York City; their Web site is www.kalustyan.com. One of them is Frontier brand, from the Frontier Co-op in Norway, Iowa (www .frontiercoop.com); it is called a flavor, not an extract. Alcohol free and oil based, it contains other natural flavors. I believe I can detect a slight hint of pineapple taste, which is a nice addition, because it gives it an overall tropical aroma and flavor. The other is Cock Brand, a coconut essence from Bangkok, Thailand. True, it doesn't say "pure" on the label, but it does not say "imitation" either. There may be other good-quality extracts out there, but I have not been able to find them. If you know of one, I would appreciate hearing from you. Because it is difficult to find, I call for coconut extract in only a few recipes in this book. If you happen to have some on hand and want to increase the coconut flavor of other desserts, add it very carefully, starting with a very small amount

and slowly adjusting it to taste. Coconut flavorings, essences, and extracts are not standardized as vanilla extract is, so you must always be careful not to overwhelm a dish with their flavor.

BAKING BASICS

It's most important that you have fun, enjoy what you are doing, and not be anxious about the results. If your first efforts are not perfect to look at, you will find the encouragement to try again when everyone who tastes them raves about how delicious they are. You need not be a dedicated or experienced cook to produce delicious results.

All the recipes in this book are tried and tested, and changing the ingredients or methods will give different results. I suggest you follow the recipes carefully to begin with, and you will soon discover for yourself those that can easily be varied and how you might want to vary them.

Read the entire recipe before you begin. Then assemble the ingredients and equipment. Check to see if any ingredients need to be at room temperature before beginning.

Always use the best-quality ingredients.

Use the appropriate measuring cups for dry and liquid ingredients. For liquids, use glass measuring cups with spouts. For dry ingredients, use metal cups that can be leveled off with a knife or spatula.

Preheat the oven for at least 15 minutes before baking. Be sure your oven temperature is correct; if it isn't, the baking time given in the recipes won't be reliable. Check the oven temperature often, using a mercury-type oven thermometer set on the middle oven rack. After preheating the oven, check the thermometer. If the temperature setting disagrees with the reading on the thermometer, adjust it up or down accordingly. Baked goods should be baked in the middle of the oven unless otherwise indicated.

Most cakes, pies, and tarts should be cooled on wire racks (in or out of the pan, depending on the recipe) to prevent the bottom of the dessert from becoming soggy.

INGREDIENTS

BAKING POWDER AND BAKING SODA

Baking soda, pure bicarbonate of soda, is activated when it is mixed with an ingredient that is acidic, such as buttermilk. Baking powder, a combination of bicarbonate of soda, cream of tartar, and cornstarch, works no matter what liquid it's mixed with, as the cream of tartar provides the acidity. Don't let a batter made with baking powder or soda sit around before baking it, or you may not get optimal service from the leavener. Check the expiration dates on the packages before using and be precise in your measuring, as too little or too much will not give the desired result.

BUTTER

Opt for the fullness of flavor and the creaminess of butter when making these desserts. Margarine doesn't taste good, it has an unpleasant mouth-feel, and it is loaded with trans fats (the most unhealthful fats of all). Use unsalted, or sweet, butter for these recipes; salted butter is too salty for coconut desserts. (If you are observing Jewish dietary laws, you will want to substitute parve margarine for butter for nondairy meals. If you must use margarine instead of butter, use it in its least processed state; that is, don't use tub margarine, spreads, or butter substitutes, which contain more water than stick margarine and are not made for baking.) When a recipe calls for cutting the butter into small pieces, cut it into about ¼-inch pieces.

EGGS

Use fresh Grade AA large eggs for these recipes; using a different size may mean disappointing results. Always purchase eggs from a refrigerated case and keep them refrigerated at home.

MANGO

Is there a better combination than mango and coconut? The mango is the most consumed fruit in the world, and it is probably the best loved of all tropical fruits. There are more than one thousand different varieties of mangoes, and the flavor differs depending on variety and stage of ripeness. Choosing a mango by fragrance is a good idea—if it doesn't smell good, it probably won't taste good. A fully ripe mango will have a luscious fruity aroma at the stem end and be soft to the touch. Mangoes vary widely in color depending on variety and their exposure to sunlight, so you can't use color as an indicator of ripeness. Ripen mangoes at room temperature.

Conventional wisdom says the mango is native to South and Southeast Asia. Most of the mangoes currently sold in the United States are imported from Mexico, Haiti, the Caribbean, or South America, but the fabulous Indian mangoes are now arriving in our markets. Their flavor is very sweet.

:• CANNED SWEETENED
   MANGO PUREE

Canned sweetened mango puree is a delicious and very convenient product from South Asia. (It's what they use to make those mango lassis you enjoy in your favorite Indian restaurant.) There are no fibers in the puree, and it has an intense fresh flavor. Try Swad or Ratnā brands, available in Asian markets.

How to Cut Up a Mango

1. Cut the mango in half, cutting down either side of the flat seed, with a sharp knife.

2. Cut the flesh of each half into squares or diamonds, the size depending on the recipe, by scoring it with a sharp knife, without cutting through the skin. Turn each mango half inside out and slice off the cubes from the skin.

Nuts of all sorts marry delightfully with coconut. Unfortunately, nuts can turn rancid quickly. For a longer shelf life, buy whole nuts and store in self-sealing plastic bags in the freezer, where they will keep for up to 6 months. Toast nuts before using them to bring out their flavor and a wonderful crunch. Always taste nuts before using them; a rancid nut will ruin a dessert.

Known as the vanilla of Asia, the pandan, or screw-pine leaf, is at least that aromatic. Used mostly to flavor sweet dishes and drinks, the leaves can be difficult to find fresh in the United States. When you do find a source, for either frozen or fresh leaves, generally a Southeast Asian market, pick up a stash and keep them in your freezer. Their flavor and aroma is fresh, green, and almost perfumed. Because you will usually be adding them to a steeping liquid and they will be strained out later, all you need to do is bruise the leaves with a knife, or tie them in knots, before using to bring out the most flavor. The coconut stalls in markets in Asia frequently also sell pandan leaves because they go well with coconut and the two are so often used together.

How to Peel and Remove the Eyes of a Pineapple

1. Cut off the top and bottom of the pineapple with a sharp knife.

2. Stand the fruit on end on a cutting board. Following the contours of the fruit, carefully and evenly cut away the peel, one long strip at a time, from top to bottom. Be careful not to cut too deeply into the flesh.

3. If you look at the pineapple, you will see that the eyes are lined up in spirals around the fruit. Working row by row, remove the eyes three or four at a time by cutting out shallow V-shaped wedges of fruit.

PURE VANILLA EXTRACT AND PASTE

There is no quicker way to ruin a dessert than by using strong, artificially flavored extracts. Vanilla—and other extracts, including coconut—must be the real thing. In simple, luscious coconut desserts, the vanilla you use is especially important. You want good complex flavor and the aroma of fine vanilla, from the fruit of the vanilla orchid. If you prefer to use vanilla beans rather than extract, you might consider trying pure vanilla paste. It is a blend of pure concentrated extract and beans, including the seeds, in a natural sugar syrup, and it is easily measured. Give it a try, especially if you find the look of the tiny seeds in your desserts irresistible. Nielsen-Massey makes one with beans from Madagascar that is available at specialty foods stores and many supermarkets. None of the recipes in this book call for vanilla beans. The beans are incredibly expensive at the moment (and how much vanilla sugar can you make with the leftover pods?). I love the flavor and the flecks of little seeds, but my preference is for high-quality pure vanilla extract and vanilla paste.

It's best to add pure vanilla paste or extract to cool ingredients, because they both have an alcohol base, and heat will release not only the fragrance, but the flavor as well.

EQUIPMENT

BAKING PANS

Use shiny, not dark, baking pans. Baking sheets should fit into the oven with at least 2 inches of space between them and the oven walls so the heat can circulate freely.

BLOWTORCH

A small kitchen blowtorch, available at many kitchenware shops, including Williams-Sonoma, is perfect for caramelizing the sugar on the Coconut Crème Brûlée Tart (page 55). It gives you much more control than using a broiler, and the flame melts the sugar quickly, so the custard does not overcook. It is compact, has a comfortable rubber handle, and uses readily available butane fuel.

ELECTRIC MIXERS

My friend Marie gave me a wonderful gift—a stand mixer. I love it and use it often. But if you don't have one, you can use a handheld mixer for any of these recipes with great results; mixing will just take a little longer.

GLASS MEASURES

I use medium (4-cup) and large (8-cup) glass measures over and over when making desserts. Besides measuring with them, you can strain a custard or similar mixture into one of these, making it very easy to pour it into ramekins, baking dishes, or an ice-cream maker. And, if you're not comfortable slowly pouring hot half-and-half or cream directly from the saucepan into a bowl of beaten eggs or yolks when making custard, because the pan is heavy or doesn't have a spout, pour it into a glass measure and then into the eggs.

ICE-CREAM MAKERS

There are now many reasonably priced machines available that don't require the messy use of salt and ice, making the preparation of frozen desserts easy enough for a school night. Look for one that makes at least 1 quart.

MICROPLANE

The Microplane rasp grater's razor-sharp teeth shave lime and other citrus zest instead of ripping and shredding it, and it removes a lot more of the zest than other graters and gadgets. It also seems to never remove the white pith, which is a minor miracle in itself (that bitter white pith may be great for making marmalade set, because it contains a lot of pectin, but it can ruin a luscious coconut dessert). The Microplane is very comfortable to hold and use, with a well-balanced design, like a good knife. Once you use one, you'll never go back. These are widely available in kitchenware stores; for more information, go to www.microplane.com. If you've ever left zest out of a recipe because you thought it was too much trouble, give the Microplane a go.

MIXING BOWLS

It's impossible to have too many mixing bowls. Stainless-steel bowls are great for using as an improvised double boiler over a saucepan of hot water. Glass bowls are essential for use in the microwave, for melting chocolate or butter. For dessert making, you'll need at least one very large bowl for beating egg whites, cream, and the like. I find deep bowls far more versatile than shallower ones.

PROBE OR CANDY THERMOMETER

A probe thermometer is very handy when making candy or deep-frying the Coconut-Fried Bananas on page 105. You can leave the thermometer right in the saucepan, so you always know the exact temperature of the oil or other mixture, and it doesn't get

in the way. You can even set an alarm to go off when your mixture reaches the temperature you're looking for.

ROLLING PIN

The type you use is really a matter of personal taste—whatever you feel comfortable with. Your grandmother's pin, a wooden dowel type, or a heavy ball-bearing pin with handles: any of these will be great.

RUBBER SPATULAS

One of the greatest recent advances in kitchen equipment is the development of heat-resistant rubber spatulas. Not having to worry about a meltdown is quite wonderful. Now you can use rubber spatulas for cooking, as well as for scraping down bowls while mixing, folding ingredients, and many other tasks. My new favorite rubber spatulas are from Martha Stewart, sold at Macy's and online. These are made from one piece of silicone, not with a separate handle and blade, so they are easy to clean.

SIFTER

I don't use a sifter for sifting; I use a coarse strainer. Use whichever you like, but for accurate measuring and the best crumb in your baked goods, don't skip the sifting step when a recipe calls for it.

SILICONE BAKING MAT

I recommend using a silicone baking mat for many of the cookies (and some of the other recipes) in this book, to keep them from sticking to the baking sheet. I usually give other alternatives, but I like the silicone mats best. And when I don't list another option, there isn't one. The most common brand is Silpat from France, which can be found in kitchenware stores. For cookies especially, it is useful to have two of them. You'll find many uses for yours once you have them in your kitchen.

STRAINERS

I use strainers often, to strain out coconut and whatever else might get in the way of the perfect smoothness of a finished custard or similar dessert. Have a few on hand, large and small, coarse and fine. A small fine strainer is also perfect for sifting confectioners' sugar or cocoa powder over a dessert just before serving.

WHISKS

These are very handy kitchen tools. Find one or two that feel well balanced and comfortable in your hand. I often use a whisk to aerate and mix dry ingredients; it's quicker and easier than sifting when sifting is not really necessary. I also use whisks for folding one component of a dish into another. Have both large and small whisks on hand, but I find smaller, more flexible whisks best for most tasks.

WIRE RACKS

A couple of large, sturdy wire racks are essential for cooling baked goods.

TIPS, TECHNIQUES, AND TRICKS OF THE TRADE

BEATING EGG WHITES

Always use an impeccably clean bowl and beaters. If I'm not absolutely confident that no vestige of egg yolk or other fat is lurking, I give the beaters and bowl a quick wash with a bit of vinegar and water. I've found it works best to beat at medium speed until the whites are foamy, then increase the speed to medium-high and beat to soft or stiff peaks as the recipe requires. For soft peaks, beat the whites just until when the mixer is turned off and the beaters are lifted, the foam makes a peak that falls over immediately. For stiff peaks, beat until that peak stands straight up and stays there.

COOKING TIMES

When a range of cooking or baking times is given (for example, "Bake for 30 to 40 minutes"), always check for doneness after the first increment of time has elapsed and then continue to watch closely until done.

CREAMING BUTTER AND SUGAR

Use an electric mixer for creaming butter and sugar and beat until the sugar is barely grainy and the mixture is light and fluffy. This can take a few minutes, so make sure to beat long enough. Begin with room-temperature butter.

CUTTING OUT BISCUITS

Pat out the dough to the desired thickness. Dip the biscuit cutter into flour and cut out the biscuits using a straight in-and-out motion, dipping the cutter into the flour again before cutting out each biscuit. Then gather together and pat out the scraps if necessary to cut out more biscuits.

FOLDING

Folding is used to combine certain ingredients, such as whipped egg whites, with another ingredient or mixture without deflating them. For most recipes, you can use either a whisk or a rubber spatula. First add a small amount of the mixture you're folding in to the bowl and cut straight down through the center of the mixture to incorporate it, then turn the whisk or spatula toward you and lift up. Turn the bowl an inch or two and repeat, working around the bowl just until no streaks remain. Then add the remainder and fold in.

MEASURING BROWN SUGAR

Firmly pack the sugar into a metal measuring cup, pressing down on it firmly enough so that it will hold its shape when turned out. Use a small metal spatula or a table knife to level off the top.

MEASURING FLOUR

The way you measure flour for a dessert recipe is crucial to the final outcome. For these recipes, first stir the flour in the canister to aerate it, then spoon it into the measuring cup so that it mounds above the top and level the top with a metal spatula or table knife. (Always use a metal measuring cup for dry ingredients.) Dipping the measuring cup into the flour and scooping it out will give you a different amount of flour, and your results may be disappointing. Another flour caveat: 1 cup flour, sifted, is different enough from 1 cup sifted flour to affect the dessert. Pay close attention to whether the flour should be sifted before measuring or after, or both.

ROLLING OUT PIE OR TART PASTRY

Place the disk of dough on a lightly floured smooth work surface and sprinkle the dough and the rolling pin with flour. Roll out the dough with short, even strokes, working from the center out, lifting and turning the pastry as you roll. To transfer the pastry to the pie or tart pan, carefully fold it over the rolling pin, lift it up, and drape it over the pan, then ease it gently into the pan without stretching it. For sticky or hard-to-handle doughs, flour a piece of wax paper and put the disk of dough on it, flour the dough, and place another sheet of wax paper over the dough before rolling it out. Using wax paper is also good if crusts make you nervous and you need to build your confidence.

STRAINING

To strain a custard, puree, or other mixture, I find it's best to use two heatproof rubber spatulas—one inside the strainer, for pushing ingredients through, and a second one for scraping the bottom of the strainer to get everything that has been strained.

CAKES

We coconut lovers are cake lovers too, and cakes are one of the best showcases for coconut.

Included here are the classics, with some fun and interesting twists. For example, my version of German Chocolate (Not) Cupcakes (page 47) is made with dark chocolate, which adds more chocolate flavor and is a much better counterpoint to the luscious, gooey coconut and pecan mixture that graces the top of the cupcakes. Pineapple upside-down cake is another classic, but it doesn't usually include coconut. But you will find a light and tasty Pineapple-Coconut-Ginger Upside-Down Cake (page 42) that includes toasted coconut and ginger in the batter. It is topped with caramelized pineapple and served warm, sprinkled with even more toasted coconut.

I am extremely fond of pound cakes, and the Coconut and Chocolate Marble Pound Cake (page 44) has lots of both coconut and chocolate flavor. The Coconut, Almond, and Lime Macaroon Cake (page 30) is a diminutive cake with a lovely peaked top glazed with coconut and sliced almonds. The exotic North African–Style Coconut and Pistachio Cake (page 40) has tons of flavor and an extraordinary moist texture from the tangerine syrup poured over it after baking. Coconut and tangerine are a terrific combination; add pistachios, and it's irresistible.

And the layer cakes—coconut layer cakes can seem like a dream, light, airy, and floating above the cake stand. You'll find a masterpiece from the Deep South, Toasted Coconut Lane Cake (page 38), rich, with complex flavors, and perfect for a celebration, frosted with what we called in my childhood home "gooey icing" (also known as seven-minute frosting), which seals in all the wonderful flavors. The Luscious Coconut Layer Cake (page 36) is prepared with fresh coconut, coconut milk, and a bit of coconut extract for a deep coconut flavor. It is topped with a simple but opulent buttercream and coated in shredded fresh coconut. The Layer Cake with Coconut and Mango Curd, Coconut, and Cream (page 33) is four layers of luscious cake flavored with lime, layered with coconut and mango curd, frosted with whipped cream, and enrobed in ribbons of fresh coconut. It is delicious!

COCONUT, ALMOND, AND LIME MACAROON CAKE

SERVES 8   Here's a pretty little cake with a lovely peaked top. Glazed with coconut and topped with sliced almonds, it has a great look. Ground almonds, also called almond meal, can be found in specialty and health food stores. You can also make your own in a food processor.

CAKE

2 CUPS ALL-PURPOSE FLOUR

½ CUP SHREDDED UNSWEETENED DRIED COCONUT

⅓ CUP GROUND ALMONDS

½ TEASPOON BAKING POWDER

¼ TEASPOON SALT

1 CUP (2 STICKS) UNSALTED BUTTER, AT ROOM TEMPERATURE

1 CUP SUGAR

2 TEASPOONS FINELY GRATED LIME ZEST

4 LARGE EGGS, AT ROOM TEMPERATURE

1 LARGE EGG YOLK

½ TEASPOON PURE VANILLA EXTRACT

TOPPING

1 LARGE EGG WHITE

¼ CUP SHREDDED UNSWEETENED DRIED COCONUT

⅓ CUP GROUND ALMONDS

⅓ CUP TURBINADO SUGAR (SEE COOK'S NOTE, PAGE 32)

⅓ CUP SLICED ALMONDS

1. To make the cake: Position a rack in the middle of the oven and preheat the oven to 350°F. Butter an 8- or 8½-inch springform pan and line the bottom of the pan with parchment or wax paper.

2. Stir together the flour, coconut, ground almonds, baking powder, and salt with a fork in a medium bowl until well combined.

3. Beat the butter, sugar, and lime zest with an electric mixer on medium-high speed in a large deep bowl until light and fluffy. Add the eggs and yolk one at a time, beating well after each addition and scraping down the side of the bowl as necessary (the mixture may look curdled, but it will come together). Beat in the vanilla. Reduce the speed to low and add the flour mixture in three batches, scraping down the side of the bowl as necessary, and beating just until blended; the batter will be thick. Transfer the batter to the springform pan and smooth the top with a rubber spatula.

4. To make the topping: Whisk the egg white in a medium bowl just until foamy. Stir in the coconut, ground almonds, and turbinado sugar. With a spoon, drop the topping onto the batter, and carefully spread it over the batter with a small offset spatula. Sprinkle with the sliced almonds.

Continued

5. Bake for 1½ hours, or until the topping is dark golden brown and a toothpick inserted in the center comes out clean. Cool completely in the pan on a wire rack.

6. Run a table knife around the edge of the pan and remove the side of the pan. Serve the cake cut into wedges (remove the parchment paper after slicing).

Cook's Note: Turbinado is pure raw cane sugar with large brown crystals and a delicate molasses flavor. If you finely grind the sugar, it will give you a smooth, glass-like top.

LAYER CAKE WITH COCONUT AND MANGO CURD, COCONUT, AND CREAM

SERVES 10 TO 12   I love a tall layer cake, and this one is very pretty. It does take some time to prepare, but you can do much of the work in advance. Make the curd and toast the coconut, then bake the cake early in the day and put it together at the last minute. If you are pressed for time, instead of fresh coconut, you can use about 2 ½ cups sweetened flaked coconut to coat the cake, but the result will be sweeter.

CAKE

2 ⅓ CUPS CAKE FLOUR (NOT SELF-RISING)

2 ¾ TEASPOONS BAKING POWDER

¼ TEASPOON SALT

1 ¾ CUPS SUGAR

¾ CUP (1 ½ STICKS) UNSALTED BUTTER, AT ROOM TEMPERATURE

1 ½ TABLESPOONS FINELY GRATED LIME ZEST

1 CUP WHOLE MILK

5 LARGE EGG WHITES, AT ROOM TEMPERATURE

¼ TEASPOON CREAM OF TARTAR

1 FRESH COCONUT

LUSCIOUS COCONUT AND MANGO CURD (PAGE 134)

1 ¼ CUPS HEAVY (WHIPPING) CREAM

2 TABLESPOONS CONFECTIONERS' SUGAR

1. To make the cake: Position a rack in middle of the oven and preheat the oven to 350°F. Generously butter and flour two 8-by-2-inch round cake pans.

2. Whisk together the flour, baking powder, and salt in a medium bowl.

3. Beat the sugar, butter, and lime zest with an electric mixer on medium-high speed in a large deep bowl until light and fluffy. Add ¼ cup of the milk and beat just until blended. Reduce the speed to low and add the flour mixture alternately with the remaining ¾ cup milk in two batches, scraping down the sides of the bowl as necessary and beating just until blended.

4. Beat the egg whites with clean beaters on medium speed in a large deep bowl just until foamy. Add the cream of tartar, increase the speed to medium-high, and beat just until the egg whites hold stiff peaks when the beaters are lifted. With a whisk or a rubber spatula, fold one-third of the egg whites into the batter to lighten it, then fold in the remaining egg whites.

5. Divide the batter evenly between the prepared pans and smooth the tops with a rubber spatula.

Continued

Bake for 35 to 40 minutes, until a toothpick inserted in the centers comes out clean. Cool in the pans on wire racks for 10 minutes. (Leave the oven on if you are planning to toast the coconut, and adjust the racks so they are in the upper and lower thirds of the oven.) Run a table knife around the sides of the pans, and carefully turn the cakes out onto the racks to cool completely.

6. Meanwhile, open the coconut, remove the meat from the shell, and remove the peel with a vegetable peeler (see page 9). Rinse the coconut and dry with paper towels. Cut enough coconut into ribbons with a vegetable peeler (see page 10) to measure 2½ cups (reserve the remaining coconut for another use). If you want to toast the coconut, follow the directions on page 10.

7. Cut each cake into two layers with a long serrated knife. Place one cake layer on a serving plate. Spread with one-third of the coconut and mango curd, spreading it to about ½ inch from the edges. Repeat with two more cake layers and top with the fourth layer.

8. Beat the cream with an electric mixer on medium-high speed in a large deep bowl until it holds soft peaks when the beaters are lifted. Add the confectioners' sugar and beat until the cream holds stiff peaks when the beaters are lifted.

9. Frost the top and the sides of the cake with the whipped cream. Using your palms, press some of the coconut onto the sides of the cake and cover the top with the remaining coconut. Serve immediately, cut into wedges.

LUSCIOUS COCONUT LAYER CAKE

Who doesn't love a luscious coconut layer cake? This one is particularly delightful, with a simple but rich buttercream, a fresh coconut coating, and cake that fairly melts in your mouth. Don't be put off by the thought of using fresh coconut instead of packaged. For a special occasion, it is truly worth the effort. You can use the seven-minute frosting for the Toasted Coconut Lane Cake (page 38) rather than the buttercream if you prefer.

CAKE

1 FRESH COCONUT

2 ¼ CUPS CAKE FLOUR (NOT SELF-RISING)

2 TEASPOONS BAKING POWDER

½ TEASPOON SALT

¾ CUP (1 ½ STICKS) UNSALTED BUTTER, AT ROOM TEMPERATURE

1 ⅓ CUPS SUGAR

2 LARGE EGGS, AT ROOM TEMPERATURE

1 TEASPOON PURE VANILLA EXTRACT

¾ TEASPOON PURE COCONUT EXTRACT

1 CUP FRESH OR WELL-STIRRED CANNED UNSWEETENED COCONUT MILK

FROSTING

2 LARGE EGG WHITES, AT ROOM TEMPERATURE

½ CUP SUGAR

¾ CUP (1 ½ STICKS) UNSALTED BUTTER, CUT INTO 12 PIECES, AT ROOM TEMPERATURE

½ TEASPOON PURE VANILLA EXTRACT

1. To make the cake: Open the coconut, remove the meat from the shell, and remove the peel with a vegetable peeler (see page 9). Rinse the coconut and dry with paper towels, then cut into ½-inch pieces. With the motor running, add the coconut through the feed tube of a food processor fitted with the medium shredding disk to shred it. Measure a generous 2½ cups shredded coconut and refrigerate it, tightly covered. (Reserve any remaining coconut for another use.)

2. Position a rack in the middle of the oven and pre-heat the oven to 350°F. Butter three 8-by-1½-inch round cake pans, line the bottoms with wax paper, and butter the paper. Dust the pans with flour.

3. Whisk together the flour, baking powder, and salt in a medium bowl.

4. Beat the butter with an electric mixer on medium-high speed in a large deep bowl until light and fluffy. Add the sugar and beat until light and fluffy. Add the eggs one at a time, beating well after each addition and scraping down the sides of the bowl as necessary. Beat in the vanilla and coconut extracts. Reduce the speed to low and add the flour mixture alternately with the coconut milk in three batches, beginning and ending with the flour,

scraping down the sides of the bowl as necessary and beating just until blended. Divide the batter evenly among the prepared pans and smooth the tops with a rubber spatula.

5. Bake for about 25 minutes, or until a toothpick inserted in the centers comes out clean. Cool the cakes in the pans on wire racks for 10 minutes. Run a table knife around the sides of the pans, invert the cakes onto the racks, and remove the wax paper. Let cool completely.

6. To make the frosting: Combine the egg whites and sugar in a heatproof bowl, set it over a saucepan of about 1½ inches of barely simmering water, and heat, whisking constantly, until the mixture is warm to the touch. Transfer to a large deep bowl and beat with an electric mixer on medium-high speed until the egg whites hold soft peaks when the beaters are lifted. Increase the speed to high and add the butter one piece at a time, beating until smooth (the mixture may look curdled, but it will come together). Beat in the vanilla.

7. Place one cake layer on a serving plate. Spread a generous ½ cup of the frosting evenly over the layer. Top with the second layer and spread a generous ½ cup of the frosting evenly over it. Top with the remaining cake layer and frost the top and the sides of the cake with the remaining frosting. Using your palms, press some of the coconut onto the sides of the cake. Cover the top with the remaining coconut. Serve cut into wedges.

TOASTED COCONUT LANE CAKE

SERVES 12

Emma Rylander Lane of Clayton, Alabama, was the creator of the original Lane cake. It has evolved to include pecans and coconut, but in the original there were just raisins and "one wine glass of good whiskey or brandy." I use coconut rum, and I have also toasted the coconut in the filling, which I think makes for a better dessert. A lovely white cake with a lush filling, it improves in flavor as it ages, and it will keep for up to 2 days covered (and uncut) at cool room temperature.

CAKE

3 ½ CUPS CAKE FLOUR (NOT SELF-RISING)

1 TABLESPOON BAKING POWDER

¼ TEASPOON SALT

1 CUP WHOLE MILK, AT ROOM TEMPERATURE

1 ½ TEASPOONS PURE VANILLA EXTRACT

1 CUP (2 STICKS) UNSALTED BUTTER, AT ROOM TEMPERATURE

2 CUPS SUGAR

8 LARGE EGG WHITES, AT ROOM TEMPERATURE

FILLING

6 LARGE EGG YOLKS

¾ CUP SUGAR

¼ CUP COCONUT RUM, PREFERABLY MALIBU OR DARK RUM

6 TABLESPOONS (¾ STICK) UNSALTED BUTTER, CUT INTO 6 PIECES, AT ROOM TEMPERATURE

1. To make the cake: Position a rack in the middle of the oven and preheat the oven to 350°F. Butter and flour three round 9-by-1½-inch cake pans. Line the bottoms of the pans with parchment or wax paper.

2. Whisk together the flour, baking powder, and salt in a medium bowl. Stir together the milk and vanilla in a small bowl.

3. Beat the butter and sugar with an electric mixer on medium-high speed in a large deep bowl until light and fluffy. Reduce the speed to low and add the flour mixture and the milk mixture alternately in three batches, beginning and ending with the flour, scraping down the sides of the bowl as necessary and beating just until blended.

4. Beat the egg whites with clean beaters on medium-high speed in a large deep bowl just until they hold stiff peaks when the beaters are lifted. With a whisk or a rubber spatula, fold one-third of the egg whites into the batter to lighten it, then fold in the remaining egg whites. Divide the batter evenly among the prepared pans and smooth the tops with a rubber spatula.

¾ CUP CHOPPED PECANS

¾ CUP SHREDDED UNSWEETENED DRIED COCONUT, TOASTED (SEE PAGE 10)

¾ CUP RAISINS

FROSTING

3 LARGE EGG WHITES

1½ CUPS SUGAR

⅓ CUP WATER

1 TABLESPOON LIGHT CORN SYRUP

½ TEASPOON CREAM OF TARTAR

1 TEASPOON PURE VANILLA EXTRACT

5. Bake for 20 to 25 minutes, until a toothpick inserted in the centers comes out clean. Cool the cakes in the pans on wire racks for 10 minutes. (Leave the oven on.) Run a table knife around the sides of the pans, invert the cakes onto the racks, and remove the parchment paper. Let cool completely.

6. To make the filling: Whisk together the egg yolks and sugar in a heatproof bowl, set it over a saucepan of about 1½ inches of barely simmering water, and cook, whisking constantly, for about 6 minutes, until the sugar dissolves and the mixture coats the back of a spoon. Remove the bowl from the heat and whisk in the rum. Transfer to a large deep bowl and let cool to room temperature.

7. Beat the egg mixture with an electric mixer on medium-high speed until very thick and pale. Beat in the butter one piece at a time, beating until smooth and creamy after each addition. With a rubber spatula, fold in the pecans, toasted coconut, and raisins.

8. To make the frosting: Combine the egg whites, sugar, water, corn syrup, and cream of tartar in a large deep heatproof bowl, set it over the saucepan of barely simmering water, and beat with an electric mixer on high speed for about 7 minutes, until the mixture holds soft peaks when the beaters are lifted. Remove the bowl from the heat, beat in the vanilla, and beat on high speed until the frosting has cooled to room temperature and is very stiff.

9. Place one cake layer on a serving plate. Spread half of the filling evenly over it with a long thin metal spatula. Top with another cake layer and spread the remaining filling over it. Top with the third cake layer. Frost the top and sides of the cake with the frosting. Serve cut into wedges.

NORTH AFRICAN–STYLE COCONUT AND PISTACHIO CAKE

SERVES 8 TO 10   This cake is topped with a hot tangerine syrup as soon as it comes out of the oven, for a moist and very flavorful treat. Choose the brightest green, most beautiful pistachios you can. They'll look much better than the brown ones with the skin on. For the ground pistachios, pulse the nuts in a food processor just until they are finely ground.

CAKE

1 ¼ CUPS SWEETENED FLAKED COCONUT

1 CUP FRESH TANGERINE JUICE (FINELY GRATE 1 ½ TEASPOONS ZEST BEFORE JUICING)

2 CUPS ALL-PURPOSE FLOUR

1 TABLESPOON GROUND CORIANDER

¼ TEASPOON BAKING POWDER

¼ TEASPOON SALT

1 CUP (2 STICKS) UNSALTED BUTTER, AT ROOM TEMPERATURE

¼ CUP SUGAR

4 LARGE EGGS, AT ROOM TEMPERATURE

1 CUP GROUND PISTACHIOS, PLUS ¼ CUP COARSELY CHOPPED PISTACHIOS

SYRUP

⅔ CUP FRESH TANGERINE JUICE

6 TABLESPOONS SUGAR

1. To make the cake: Position a rack in the middle of the oven and preheat the oven to 325°F. Butter a 9-inch springform pan, line the bottom with parchment or wax paper, and butter the paper.

2. Stir together the coconut and 1 cup tangerine juice in a medium bowl. Whisk together the flour, coriander, baking powder, and salt in another medium bowl.

3. Beat the butter, sugar, and tangerine zest with an electric mixer on medium-high speed in a large deep bowl until light and fluffy. Add the eggs one at a time, beating well after each addition (the mixture may look curdled, but it will come together). Reduce the speed to low and add the flour mixture in three batches, scraping down the sides of the bowl as necessary and beating just until blended. With a rubber spatula, stir in the coconut mixture and ground pistachios. Transfer the batter to the pan and smooth the top with a rubber spatula. Sprinkle with the chopped pistachios.

4. Bake for 45 to 50 minutes, until a toothpick inserted in the center comes out clean. Set the pan on a wire rack.

5. To make the syrup: Bring the ⅔ cup tangerine juice and sugar to a boil in a medium saucepan over medium-high heat, stirring until the sugar is dissolved. Increase the heat to high and boil the syrup for 4 to 5 minutes, until slightly thickened.

6. Pour the hot syrup over the hot cake. Let the cake cool completely in the pan on the wire rack.

7. Run a table knife around the edge of the pan to loosen the cake and remove the side of the pan. Serve the cake cut into wedges (remove the parchment paper after slicing).

PINEAPPLE-COCONUT-GINGER UPSIDE-DOWN CAKE

SERVES 8

Until relatively recently, pineapples were only available to those who lived in the tropics and to very wealthy Europeans, and so they were known as the fruit of kings. It was only with the advent of air transport that fresh Hawaiian pineapple began to arrive in mainland markets. Select pineapples that are fresh looking and heavy for their size. Avoid fruit that is bruised or has brown leaves or soft spots. Smell the pineapple—if it smells good, it will likely taste good. (Many people think that if you can easily pull a leaf out of the crown, the pineapple is ripe, but that test doesn't really tell you anything.) Once you have your first-rate pineapple, you can make this first-rate upside-down cake. Serve it with whipped crème fraîche or heavy cream.

1 RIPE PINEAPPLE, PEELED AND EYES REMOVED (SEE PAGE 22)

1 CUP SHREDDED UNSWEETENED DRIED COCONUT, TOASTED (SEE PAGE 10)

1 CUP GRANULATED SUGAR

2 TABLESPOONS CHOPPED CRYSTALLIZED GINGER

1 ½ CUPS ALL-PURPOSE FLOUR

2 TEASPOONS BAKING POWDER

¼ TEASPOON SALT

¾ CUP (1 ½ STICKS) UNSALTED BUTTER, AT ROOM TEMPERATURE

¼ CUP PACKED DARK BROWN SUGAR

2 LARGE EGGS, SEPARATED, AT ROOM TEMPERATURE

¾ TEASPOON PURE VANILLA EXTRACT

½ CUP FRESH OR WELL-STIRRED CANNED UNSWEETENED COCONUT MILK

¼ TEASPOON CREAM OF TARTAR

1. Position a rack in the middle of the oven and preheat the oven to 350°F.

2. Lay the pineapple on its side and cut, crosswise, six ⅜-inch-thick slices from it. (Reserve the remaining pineapple for another use.) Cut each slice crosswise in half. With a small sharp knife, remove the core from each slice.

3. Process ¾ cup of the toasted coconut, ½ cup of the granulated sugar, and the ginger in a food processor until the coconut and ginger are finely ground.

4. Whisk together the flour, baking powder, and salt in a medium bowl.

5. Melt ¼ cup of the butter with the brown sugar in an ovenproof 10-inch nonstick skillet over medium heat, stirring until the sugar is dissolved. Add the pineapple, increase the heat to high, bring to a boil, and boil for 3 minutes, gently turning the pineapple. Remove the skillet from the heat; there will be a lot of liquid. Arrange the pineapple slices attractively in the skillet.

6. Beat the remaining ½ cup butter with an electric mixer on medium-high speed in a large deep bowl until light and fluffy. Add the coconut-sugar mixture and the remaining ½ cup granulated sugar and beat until light and fluffy, scraping down the sides of the bowl as necessary (this will take longer than usual because of the coconut). Add the egg yolks and vanilla and beat until blended. Reduce the speed to low and add the flour mixture alternately with the coconut milk in two batches, scraping down the sides of the bowl as necessary and beating just until blended.

7. Beat the egg whites with clean beaters on medium speed in a medium deep bowl just until foamy. Increase the speed to medium-high, add the cream of tartar, and beat just until the egg whites hold stiff peaks when the beaters are lifted. With a whisk or a rubber spatula, fold one-quarter of the whites into the batter to lighten it, then fold in the remaining whites one-quarter at a time. The batter will be thick.

8. Spoon the batter over the pineapple in the skillet and gently smooth the top with a rubber spatula; the batter will spread to completely cover the pineapple during baking. Bake for 55 to 60 minutes, until the top is dark golden brown and a toothpick inserted in the center comes out clean. Let cool in the skillet on a wire rack for 15 minutes.

9. Run a rubber spatula around the edges of the cake and invert it onto a large heatproof serving platter. Leave the skillet over the cake for 5 minutes, then remove it. Cool the cake until warm.

10. Top the cake with the remaining toasted coconut. Serve warm, cut into wedges.

COCONUT AND CHOCOLATE MARBLE POUND CAKE

SERVES 10 TO 12   Natural cocoa powder is cocoa that does not have an alkali added (or is not "Dutched" as it is sometimes called). Scharffen Berger and Dagoba both make an excellent natural cocoa powder; Hershey's makes both styles, which are available in any supermarket. I call for coconut extract here so the cake will have lots of coconut flavor.

---

3 TABLESPOONS SUGAR PLUS 2 CUPS

¼ CUP NATURAL UNSWEETENED COCOA POWDER

¼ CUP WATER

2 TABLESPOONS LIGHT CORN SYRUP

⅛ TEASPOON BAKING SODA

3 CUPS ALL-PURPOSE FLOUR

½ TEASPOON BAKING POWDER

½ TEASPOON SALT

1 ¾ CUPS (3 ½ STICKS) UNSALTED BUTTER, AT ROOM TEMPERATURE

5 LARGE EGGS, AT ROOM TEMPERATURE

1 CUP FRESH OR WELL-STIRRED CANNED UNSWEETENED COCONUT MILK

1 CUP SWEETENED FLAKED COCONUT

1 ½ TEASPOONS PURE COCONUT EXTRACT

CONFECTIONERS' SUGAR FOR DUSTING

1. Position a rack in the middle of the oven and pre-heat the oven to 325°F. Generously butter and flour a 10-inch Bundt pan.

2. Combine the 3 tablespoons sugar, the cocoa powder, water, and corn syrup in a small saucepan and bring just to a boil over medium heat, stirring until the sugar is dissolved. Transfer to a medium bowl and let cool to room temperature. Stir in the baking soda.

3. Whisk together the flour, baking powder, and salt in a medium bowl.

4. Beat the butter with an electric mixer on medium-high speed in a large deep bowl until light and fluffy. Gradually add the remaining 2 cups sugar and beat until light and fluffy, scraping down the sides of the bowl as necessary. Add the eggs one at a time, beating well after each addition and scraping down the sides of the bowl as necessary. Reduce the speed to low and add the flour mixture and the coconut milk alternately in three batches, beginning and ending with the flour, scraping down the sides of the bowl as necessary and beating just until blended.

Continued

5. Add 1 cup of the batter to the cocoa mixture and whisk until blended. Whisk the flaked coconut and coconut extract into the remaining batter. Spoon three-quarters of the coconut batter into the Bundt pan. Spoon a ring of cocoa batter over the coconut batter, just in the center; do not spread it to the edges. Spoon the remaining coconut batter on top. With a long thin knife, gently swirl the batters to marbleize them.

6. Bake for 1 hour and 25 to 30 minutes, until a toothpick inserted in the center comes out clean. Cool in the pan on a wire rack for 15 minutes, then invert the cake onto the rack and cool completely. Dust with the confectioners' sugar and serve cut into slices.

GERMAN CHOCOLATE (NOT) CUPCAKES

MAKES 12 CUPCAKES This has the same flavors as a classic German chocolate cake, but it is made with dark, rich bittersweet chocolate instead of sweet chocolate. There's nothing German about German chocolate cake—it is named for the German sweet chocolate that is used to make it. The chocolate is called "German" because Dr. James Baker, who financed the first American chocolate factory, hired Samuel German to develop a sweet chocolate. I love the contrast of dark chocolate with the sticky, gooey, sweet pecan and coconut confection. Don't use a "high-percentage" chocolate here, though; keep it below 60 percent.

CUPCAKES

2 OUNCES BITTERSWEET OR SEMISWEET CHOCOLATE, FINELY CHOPPED

¼ CUP BOILING WATER

1 CUP PLUS 1 TABLESPOON CAKE FLOUR (NOT SELF-RISING)

1 TABLESPOON NATURAL UNSWEETENED COCOA POWDER

½ TEASPOON BAKING SODA

¼ TEASPOON SALT

½ CUP (1 STICK) UNSALTED BUTTER, AT ROOM TEMPERATURE

¾ CUP SUGAR

2 LARGE EGGS, SEPARATED, AT ROOM TEMPERATURE

½ TEASPOON PURE VANILLA EXTRACT

½ CUP BUTTERMILK, AT ROOM TEMPERATURE

Continued

1. To make the cupcakes: Position a rack in the middle of the oven and preheat the oven to 350°F. Line 12 muffin cups with paper or foil liners.

2. Whisk together the chocolate and boiling water in a medium bowl until the chocolate is melted and the mixture is smooth. Let cool to room temperature.

3. Whisk together the flour, cocoa powder, baking soda, and salt in a medium bowl.

4. Beat the butter and sugar with an electric mixer on medium-high speed in a large deep bowl until light and fluffy. Add the egg yolks and beat until well combined. Gradually beat in the chocolate mixture and then the vanilla until smooth, scraping down the sides of the bowl as necessary. Reduce the speed to low and add the flour mixture and the buttermilk alternately in three batches, beginning and ending with the flour, scraping down the side of the bowl as necessary and beating just until blended.

Continued

FROSTING

¾ CUP EVAPORATED MILK

¼ CUP PACKED LIGHT BROWN SUGAR

2 LARGE EGG YOLKS

LARGE PINCH OF SALT

2 TABLESPOONS UNSALTED BUTTER, AT ROOM TEMPERATURE

2 OUNCES BITTERSWEET OR SEMISWEET CHOCOLATE, FINELY CHOPPED

1 ½ CUPS SWEETENED FLAKED COCO-NUT, PLUS MORE FOR GARNISH

1 CUP CHOPPED PECANS

½ TEASPOON PURE VANILLA EXTRACT

5. Beat the egg whites with clean beaters on medium-high speed in a medium deep bowl until the whites hold stiff peaks when the beaters are lifted. With a whisk or a rubber spatula, fold one-quarter of the egg whites into the chocolate mixture to lighten it, then fold in the remaining whites.

6. Divide the batter evenly among the paper-lined muffin cups. Bake for 25 minutes, or until the cupcakes spring back when touched lightly in the center. Let cool in the pans for 5 minutes, then transfer the cupcakes to wire racks, right-side up, to cool completely.

7. To make the frosting: Whisk together the evaporated milk, brown sugar, egg yolks, and salt just until smooth in a medium heavy saucepan. Put the saucepan over medium heat, add the butter, and cook, whisking constantly, for about 5 minutes, until the butter has melted and the mixture is slightly thickened; do not let the mixture boil. Remove the saucepan from the heat, add the chocolate, and whisk until the chocolate is melted and the mixture is smooth. With a rubber spatula, stir in the 1½ cups coconut, pecans, and vanilla. Let cool to room temperature.

8. Spread the tops of the cupcakes with the frosting. Sprinkle with more coconut before serving.

A PIE, A MULTITUDE OF TARTS, AND A CHEESECAKE

Look no further for a great coconut cream pie.

The one in this chapter, Classic Toasted Coconut Cream Pie (page 52), is made with a rich toasted coconut pastry cream that is nestled in a flaky crust and topped with billowy whipped cream and toasted coconut. There is also a Mango Cheesecake Enrobed in Coconut Praline (page 63)—a very creamy cheesecake flavored with lime and completely coated in crushed coconut praline. The praline elevates the cheesecake into the sublime, and it is a showstopper. Because coconut combines so very well with chocolate, you will find a Bittersweet Chocolate and Coconut Tart (page 61). It is perfectly simple yet elegant; there are options for dolling it up a bit, but only if you want to. The Coconut Crème Brûlée Tart (page 55) would be the hit of any dinner party or celebration.

The rich toasted coconut custard inside a short crisp crust is topped with thin-as-glass caramelized sugar. The Macadamia and Coconut Tart (page 58), baked in a fluted rectangular tart pan, is quite beautiful. The filling is made with lots of coconut and coconut milk, sweet butter, and brown sugar, and the macadamias are abundant.

CLASSIC TOASTED COCONUT CREAM PIE

SERVES 8 TO 10   This is the quintessential coconut cream pie—it has lots of coconut flavor and a very creamy texture. This is best served on the day it is made so the crust is still crisp, but you can make the pastry cream a day ahead, whisk in the whipped cream a couple of hours before serving, and then put it together at the last minute. Swirl the whipped cream decoratively on top, if you like.

CRUST

1 ⅓ CUPS ALL-PURPOSE FLOUR

2 TEASPOONS GRANULATED SUGAR

½ TEASPOON SALT

½ CUP (1 STICK) COLD UNSALTED BUTTER, CUT INTO SMALL PIECES

3 TO 4 TABLESPOONS COLD WATER

FILLING

2 ¼ CUPS FRESH OR WELL-STIRRED CANNED UNSWEETENED COCONUT MILK

⅔ CUP GRANULATED SUGAR

4 LARGE EGG YOLKS

3 TABLESPOONS ALL-PURPOSE FLOUR

2 TABLESPOONS CORNSTARCH

PINCH OF SALT

2 TABLESPOONS UNSALTED BUTTER, AT ROOM TEMPERATURE

¾ CUP PLUS 2 TABLESPOONS SHREDDED UNSWEETENED DRIED COCONUT, TOASTED (SEE PAGE 10)

¾ TEASPOON PURE VANILLA EXTRACT

1. To make the crust: Whisk together the flour, sugar, and salt in a medium bowl. Cut in the butter with a pastry blender or two knives used scissors-fashion until the butter is the size of small peas. Sprinkle 1 tablespoon of the water over the mixture, stirring with a fork to moisten it evenly. Continue adding water until the dough just begins to come together when a small bit is pressed between your fingers; do not overwork the dough. Press the dough together into a ball and knead lightly. Shape the dough into a disk, wrap in wax paper, and refrigerate for at 30 minutes, or for up to 2 days.

2. Position a rack in the middle of the oven and preheat the oven to 425°F.

3. Roll out the dough on a lightly floured surface to a 12- to 13-inch round. Transfer the dough to a 9-inch glass pie plate and gently press the pastry against the bottom and up the sides of the plate. Turn the overhang under and crimp the edges. Prick the bottom and sides of the shell with a fork.

4. Line the pie shell with a piece of heavy-duty aluminum foil, pressing it snugly into the bottom and against the sides, and fill with uncooked rice or beans. Bake the crust for 12 minutes. Remove the foil and rice and bake for 8 to 10 minutes longer,

Continued

Continued

1 CUP HEAVY (WHIPPING) CREAM

2 TABLESPOONS CONFECTIONERS' SUGAR

or until the crust is golden brown. Let cool to room temperature on a wire rack.

5. To make the filling: Bring the coconut milk just to a boil in a large heavy saucepan over medium heat. Remove the pan from the heat and cover to keep warm.

6. Beat the sugar and egg yolks with an electric mixer on medium-high speed in a large deep bowl until very thick and pale and the volume has increased at least three times. Reduce the speed to medium and beat in the flour, cornstarch, and salt, scraping down the sides of the bowl as necessary. While beating, gradually pour in the warm coconut milk. Return the mixture to the saucepan and cook over medium-high heat, whisking constantly, until it comes to a boil and thickens, then boil for 1 minute, whisking constantly. Remove the pan from the heat, add the butter, and whisk until melted. Add ¾ cup of the coconut and ½ teaspoon of the vanilla.

7. Transfer the pastry cream to a bowl and let cool to room temperature, whisking occasionally. Cover the surface with plastic wrap to prevent a skin from forming and refrigerate for about 2 hours, until thoroughly chilled and set, or for up to 1 day.

8. Beat the heavy cream with the confectioners' sugar with an electric mixer on medium-high speed in a large deep bowl until it holds stiff peaks when the beaters are lifted. Beat in the remaining vanilla. With a rubber spatula, fold about one-quarter of the whipped cream into the pastry cream.

9. Transfer the pastry cream to the crust and smooth the top with a small offset spatula. Spread the remaining whipped cream over the top with the clean offset spatula. Refrigerate for at least 30 minutes, or for up to 4 hours, before serving.

10. Sprinkle the top of the pie with the remaining toasted coconut. Serve cut into wedges.

COCONUT CRÈME BRÛLÉE TART

SERVES 8

You can't caramelize the sugar on top of the tart with your broiler without burning the edges of the crust, so you will need to use a small kitchen blowtorch (see page 23). If you don't have one, skip the sugar topping and instead cover the tart with finely ground Coconut Praline (page 138). This is divine served with mixed fresh berries.

CRUST

1 ⅓ CUPS ALL-PURPOSE FLOUR

1 TABLESPOON SUGAR

¼ TEASPOON SALT

½ CUP (1 STICK) COLD UNSALTED BUTTER, CUT INTO SMALL PIECES

3 TO 5 TABLESPOONS ICE WATER

FILLING

1 ½ CUPS HEAVY (WHIPPING) CREAM

1 ¼ CUPS SWEETENED FLAKED COCONUT, TOASTED (SEE PAGE 10)

¾ CUP HALF-AND-HALF

6 LARGE EGG YOLKS

2 TABLESPOONS TURBINADO SUGAR (SEE COOK'S NOTE, PAGE 32)

PINCH OF SALT

¼ CUP TURBINADO SUGAR, FINELY GROUND, IF DESIRED

1. To make the crust: Whisk together the flour, sugar, and salt in a medium bowl. Cut in the butter with a pastry blender or two knives used scissors-fashion until the butter is the size of small peas. Sprinkle 1 tablespoon of the water over the flour mixture, stirring gently with a fork to moisten it evenly. Continue adding water until the dough just begins to come together when a small bit is pressed between your fingers; do not overwork the dough. Press the dough together into a ball and knead lightly. Shape into a disk, wrap in wax paper, and refrigerate for at least 30 minutes, or for up to 2 days.

2. Roll out the dough on a lightly floured surface to a 12- to 13-inch round. Transfer the dough to a 10-inch round fluted tart pan with a removable bottom and gently press the pastry against the bottom and up the sides. Trim the pastry to about ½ inch above the edge of the pan, fold the overhang in, and gently press pastry against the sides of the pan so it extends ¼ inch above the rim. Prick the bottom and sides of the shell with a fork and refrigerate for 30 minutes.

3. Position a rack in the middle of the oven and preheat the oven to 350°F.

Continued

4. To make the filling: Bring the cream, toasted coconut, and half-and-half to a full boil in a large heavy saucepan over medium heat. Remove from the heat, cover, and let steep for 35 minutes.

5. Line the tart shell with a piece of heavy-duty aluminum foil, pressing it snugly into the bottom and against the sides, and fill with uncooked rice or beans. Bake the shell for 20 minutes. Remove the foil and rice and bake for about 10 minutes longer, until pale golden brown. Let cool completely on a wire rack. Lower the oven temperature to 300°F.

6. Whisk together the egg yolks, 2 tablespoons turbinado sugar, and salt in a large bowl. Slowly add the cream mixture, whisking constantly. Pour through a fine strainer set over a large glass measure, pressing hard on the solids to extract as much liquid as possible.

7. Place the tart pan on a baking sheet, put it in the oven, and pour the custard into the shell. Bake for 25 to 30 minutes, until just set; the custard will continue to set as it cools. Watch closely at the end, as it can set and overcook quickly. Remove the tart from the baking sheet and let cool completely on a wire rack.

8. Just before serving, remove the side of the tart pan. Gently blot the surface of the custard with the edge of a paper towel to remove any condensation. Sift the ¼ cup turbinado sugar evenly over the custard. Move the flame of a blowtorch evenly back and forth just above the top of the tart, avoiding the crust, until the sugar is evenly browned. Let stand for about 5 minutes before serving, cut into wedges.

MACADAMIA AND COCONUT TART

SERVES 8 TO 10   I adapted this wonderfully coconutty and nutty tart from a recipe by San Francisco pastry chef and cookbook author Emily Luchetti. I recommend serving slices of the tart with softly whipped, lightly sweetened crème fraîche or heavy cream.

CRUST

1 ½ CUPS ALL-PURPOSE FLOUR

1 TABLESPOON SUGAR

¼ TEASPOON SALT

¾ CUP (1 ½ STICKS) COLD UNSALTED BUTTER, CUT INTO SMALL PIECES

½ TEASPOON PURE VANILLA EXTRACT

2 TABLESPOONS ICE WATER

FILLING

1 CUP SWEETENED FLAKED COCONUT

1 CUP COARSELY CHOPPED MACADAMIA NUTS

¼ CUP (½ STICK) UNSALTED BUTTER

⅓ CUP PACKED LIGHT BROWN SUGAR

⅓ CUP FRESH OR WELL-STIRRED CANNED UNSWEETENED COCONUT MILK

4 LARGE EGG YOLKS

PINCH OF SALT

1. To make the crust: Whisk together the flour, sugar, and salt in a medium bowl. Cut in the butter and vanilla with a pastry blender or two knives used scissors-fashion, until the butter is the size of small peas. Sprinkle the water over the flour mixture, stirring gently with a fork to moisten it evenly. Press the dough together into a ball and knead lightly. Shape it into a 7-by-2-inch rectangle, wrap in wax paper, and refrigerate for at least 30 minutes, or for up to 2 days.

2. Roll out the dough on a lightly floured surface to a 6-by-16-inch rectangle. Transfer the dough to a 4-by-14-inch fluted rectangular tart pan with a removable bottom and gently press the pastry against the bottom and up the sides. Press the over-hang back in around the edges to make the sides of the shell a bit thicker. Prick the bottom and sides of the shell with a fork. Freeze the tart shell for at least 45 minutes (or, wrapped well, for up to 2 days).

3. Position a rack in the middle of the oven and pre-heat the oven to 400°F.

4. Bake the frozen tart shell for about 15 minutes, or until golden brown. Let cool completely on a wire rack. Lower the oven temperature to 350°F.

5. To make the filling: Spread the coconut and macadamia nuts on a large heavy baking sheet and toast in the oven, stirring twice, for 6 to 8 minutes, until golden brown. Transfer to a plate to cool completely.

6. Melt the butter in a medium heavy saucepan over medium heat. Add the brown sugar and stir just until well combined and evenly moistened. Remove the pan from the heat.

7. Whisk together the coconut milk, egg yolks, and salt in a large bowl. Whisk in the brown sugar mixture. Stir in the toasted coconut and macadamias. Transfer the mixture to the tart shell and smooth the top with a rubber spatula.

8. Place the tart pan on a baking sheet and bake for about 20 minutes, until the tart is golden brown and just set in the center. Let cool slightly on a wire rack. Remove the side of the pan and serve warm or at room temperature, cut into slices.

BITTERSWEET CHOCOLATE AND COCONUT TART

SERVES 8 TO 10   Here's an unusual way to make tart crust, processing the butter in the food processor and then adding the flour, and the result is quite wonderful, very crisp. Garnish the tart with Candied Coconut (page 141), Coconut-Caramel Popcorn (page 139), or Coconut Whipped Cream (page 140). Or keep it simple and dust it generously with unsweetened cocoa powder. You might serve it with softly whipped heavy cream or crème fraîche.

CRUST

½ CUP (1 STICK) COLD UNSALTED BUTTER, CUT INTO SMALL PIECES

¼ CUP SUGAR

½ TEASPOON PURE VANILLA EXTRACT

¼ TEASPOON SALT

1 CUP PLUS 2 TABLESPOONS ALL-PURPOSE FLOUR

FILLING

8 OUNCES BITTERSWEET OR SEMISWEET CHOCOLATE, CHOPPED

¾ TEASPOON PURE COCONUT EXTRACT (SEE PAGE 17)

1 CUP HEAVY (WHIPPING) CREAM

PINCH OF SALT

3 LARGE EGG YOLKS

1. To make the crust: Process the butter, sugar, vanilla, and salt in a food processor until smooth, scraping down the sides of the bowl as necessary. Add the flour and pulse until the mixture just begins to come together when a small amount is pinched between your fingers; do not overprocess—the dough should not form a ball. With a rubber spatula, scrape the dough out onto a lightly floured sheet of wax paper. Knead a few times, until the dough comes together, and shape it into a disk. Wrap in wax paper and refrigerate for at least 30 minutes, or for up to 2 days.

2. Flour the top and bottom of the dough and roll out between two sheets of wax paper to a 12-inch round. Peel off the top sheet of wax paper. Transfer the dough, paper-side up, to a 9-inch fluted round tart pan with a removable bottom. Peel off the paper and gently press the pastry against the bottom and up the sides. Trim the pastry to about ½ inch above the edge of the pan, fold the overhang in, and gently press the pastry against the sides of the pan so it extends ¼ inch above the rim. Prick the bottom and sides of the shell with a fork. Freeze the tart shell for at least 45 minutes (or, wrapped well, for up to 2 days).

Continued

3. Preheat the oven to 400°F.

4. Bake the frozen tart shell for 15 to 17 minutes, until deep golden brown. Let cool completely on a wire rack.

5. To make the filling: Melt the chocolate in a heat-proof bowl set over a saucepan of about 1½ inches of barely simmering water, whisking until smooth. Remove the bowl from the heat and whisk in the coconut extract.

6. Bring the cream and salt just to a boil in a medium heavy saucepan over medium-high heat. Meanwhile, whisk the egg yolks in a medium bowl. Whisking constantly, slowly pour in the hot cream mixture. Return the mixture to the saucepan and cook over medium-low heat, whisking constantly, until the custard thickens and coats the back of a spoon; if you draw your finger across the spoon, it should leave a path. Do not allow the custard to boil. Transfer to a medium bowl, add the chocolate mixture, and whisk until smooth. Let cool to room temperature.

7. Pour the filling into the tart shell. Refrigerate for at least 2 hours, until thoroughly chilled and set, or for as long as overnight.

8. Bring the tart to room temperature before serving, cut into wedges.

MANGO CHEESECAKE ENROBED IN COCONUT PRALINE

SERVES 10 TO 12   This is *soooo* creamy and wonderfully tropical. The praline is optional, but what a treat it is—the textural contrast is fantastic. Consider serving it with finely diced ripe mango.

CRUST

½ CUP SWEETENED FLAKED COCONUT, TOASTED (SEE PAGE 10)

½ CUP GRAHAM CRACKER CRUMBS

¼ CUP (½ STICK) UNSALTED BUTTER, MELTED

PINCH OF SALT

FILLING

1½ POUNDS CREAM CHEESE, AT ROOM TEMPERATURE

½ CUP SUGAR

¼ TEASPOON SALT

4 LARGE EGGS, AT ROOM TEMPERATURE

3 LARGE EGG YOLKS, AT ROOM TEMPERATURE

¾ CUP SWEETENED MANGO PUREE (SEE PAGE 20)

¼ CUP FRESH LIME JUICE

1 CUP COARSELY GROUND COCONUT PRALINE (PAGE 138)

1. To make the crust: Position a rack in the middle of the oven and preheat the oven to 325°F. Butter a 9-inch springform pan.

2. Stir together the toasted coconut, cracker crumbs, butter, and salt in a medium bowl until well combined. Press the mixture evenly over the bottom of the springform pan. Bake the crust for 10 minutes, or until set. Let cool completely on a wire rack.

3. Wrap the outside of the springform pan with heavy-duty aluminum foil. Have a roasting pan ready. Put on a kettle of water to boil for a water bath.

4. To make the filling: Beat the cream cheese with an electric mixer on medium-high speed in a large deep bowl until light and fluffy. Add the sugar and salt and beat until light and fluffy. Reduce the speed to medium and add the eggs and egg yolks one at a time, beating well after each addition and scraping down the sides of the bowl as necessary. Gradually beat in the mango puree and lime juice, scraping down the sides of the bowl as necessary.

5. Transfer the batter to the springform pan. Put the pan in the roasting pan, place in the oven, and carefully pour 1 inch of boiling water into the roasting pan. Bake for 60 to 65 minutes, until the cheesecake is puffed on the sides but still slightly

Continued

jiggly in the center. Remove from the water bath and let cool completely on a wire rack.

6. Remove the foil. Refrigerate the cheesecake, tightly covered, for at least 8 hours, until thoroughly chilled and set, or for up to 2 days.

7. Run a table knife around the edge of the pan to loosen the cheesecake, and remove the side of the pan. Using your palms, press some of the praline into the side of the cheesecake, and scatter the remaining praline over the top. Serve cold, cut into wedges.

COOKIES

There's nothing like a cookie, and coconut makes some *very* good cookies. Here you'll find four very different macaroons.

The quintessential Big Coconut Macaroons (page 71) are made with unsweetened coconut, for a macaroon that is not as sweet as others. You can dip the bottoms in dark chocolate, if you'd like. Coconut and Almond Macaroons (page 74), prepared with almond paste, have a fantastic texture, pleasing and chewy. Coconut Macaroons with Macadamia Nuts (page 75) are little cookies made with sweetened flaked coconut, and each has a macadamia nut perched on top. The Melt-in-Your-Mouth Coconut and Lime Meringue Macaroons (page 70) are composed of meringue, sweet coconut, and lots of fresh lime. They are almost weightless but packed with flavor. The Elegant Coconut and Curry Butter Cookies (page 77) are flavored with curry powder and are unique, amusing, and yummy. They are just the right cookie to have on hand to serve with a cup of tea to a friend or neighbor. And the Deep Dark Chocolate, Coconut, and Ginger Brownies (page 78) are flavored with crystallized ginger and toasted coconut. With a magnificent fudgy, smooth texture, they may become your favorite brownie of all. I tend to think of the Coconut Tuiles (page 69) as a party cookie, a special occasion cookie, but why not serve them on a weeknight next to ice cream, fruit, or any dessert, just for pleasure?

COCONUT TUILES

MAKES 10 COOKIES These crisp cookies are named *tuiles*, French for tiles, because when they are curved over a rolling pin to cool, their shape is reminiscent of French roof tiles. I use a metal ⅛ cup measure, a standard coffee measure, to measure the batter. If you like, cool the cookies over upside-down custard cups to form "bowls" to serve filled with ice cream.

¾ CUP SHREDDED UNSWEETENED DRIED COCONUT

½ CUP SUGAR

2 LARGE EGGS

¼ CUP ALL-PURPOSE FLOUR

PINCH OF SALT

1. Position a rack in the middle of the oven and preheat the oven to 350°F. Line two large heavy baking sheets with silicone baking mats. Set out a large rolling pin.

2. Stir together the coconut, sugar, eggs, flour, and salt in a medium bowl. Refrigerate the batter for 10 minutes.

3. Drop a scant 2 tablespoons batter onto one baking sheet and spread into a 5-inch circle with a small offset spatula, making sure there are no holes in the batter. Make three more circles on the baking sheet. Even the edges as necessary with the spatula.

4. Bake, turning the baking sheet around halfway through, for about 12 minutes, until the edges are golden brown. Using a wide metal spatula and pressing firmly in one quick motion, remove each tuile from the baking sheet and place over the rolling pin to cool completely. (Return the sheet to the oven if they get too firm to mold.) Meanwhile, fill the second sheet as the first one bakes, and then repeat with the remaining batter. (The cookies can be stored in an airtight container in a cool place for up to 2 days; they can be frozen for up to 1 month.)

MELT-IN-YOUR-MOUTH COCONUT AND LIME MERINGUE MACAROONS

MAKES 3 DOZEN COOKIES

These cookies are like little clouds—they have a lovely light and airy texture. You might add a large pinch of finely ground cardamom with the lime zest. And you're free to substitute another citrus zest of your choice, such as clementine or lemon. These cookies are very sweet; I like them best served with espresso.

---

2 CUPS SWEETENED FLAKED COCONUT

¼ CUP SIFTED ALL-PURPOSE FLOUR

2 TEASPOONS FINELY GRATED LIME ZEST

3 LARGE EGG WHITES, AT ROOM TEMPERATURE

PINCH OF SALT

1 ¼ CUPS SIFTED CONFECTIONERS' SUGAR

½ TEASPOON PURE VANILLA EXTRACT

1. Position a rack in the middle of the oven and preheat the oven to 325°F. Line two large heavy baking sheets with silicone baking mats or parchment paper, or use two large nonstick baking sheets.

2. Stir together the coconut, flour, and lime zest with a fork in a medium bowl until well combined.

3. Beat the egg whites and salt with an electric mixer on medium-high speed in a large deep bowl until the egg whites hold soft peaks when the beaters are lifted. Gradually add the sugar, about 1 tablespoon at a time, and beat, scraping down the sides of the bowl as necessary, just until the whites hold stiff peaks when the beaters are lifted. Beat in the vanilla.

4. With a rubber spatula, fold the coconut mixture into the meringue. Drop the batter by packed level tablespoonfuls onto the baking sheets, spacing them about 1½ inches apart.

5. Bake one sheet at a time, turning the baking sheets around halfway through, for about 20 minutes, until lightly browned and firm to the touch. Let cool completely on the baking sheets on wire racks. (The cookies can be stored in an airtight container at room temperature for up to 1 week.)

BIG COCONUT MACAROONS

**MAKES 4 DOZEN
COOKIES**

The cookies will hold the shape of the measuring spoon you use to shape them. I have both round and oval measuring spoons, so I make some round and some oval macaroons. I like the trick of the eye. Do bake the cookies right after forming them so they will keep their shape. See the variation on page 72 for directions on dipping the bottoms of the macaroons in dark chocolate; you can dip all or some of the cookies.

---

1 ½ CUPS SUGAR

5 LARGE EGG WHITES

¾ TEASPOON PURE VANILLA EXTRACT

¼ TEASPOON SALT

4 CUPS SHREDDED UNSWEETENED DRIED COCONUT

1. Position racks in the upper and lower thirds of the oven and preheat the oven to 350°F. Line two large heavy baking sheets with silicone baking mats or parchment paper, or use two large nonstick baking sheets.

2. Whisk together the sugar, egg whites, vanilla, and salt in a large bowl until well combined. Add the coconut and stir until well combined. Drop the batter by packed level tablespoons onto the baking sheets; the cookies can be placed close together because they will not spread. Smooth the cookies with damp fingers.

3. Bake the cookies, switching the pans from top to bottom and from front to back about halfway through, for 25 minutes, or until an even golden brown and dry looking. Let cool completely on the baking sheets on wire racks. (The cookies can be stored in an airtight container at room temperature for up to 1 week.)

6 OUNCES BITTERSWEET OR SEMISWEET
CHOCOLATE, FINELY CHOPPED

BIG COCONUT MACAROONS, PAGE 71

Melt the chocolate in a heatproof bowl set over a
saucepan of about 1½ inches of barely simmering
water, whisking until smooth. Remove the bowl
from the saucepan. Dip the bottoms of the cooled
macaroons into the melted chocolate, shake off
excess, and place the macaroons chocolate-side up
on wax-paper-lined baking sheets. Let stand until
the chocolate sets.

COCONUT AND ALMOND MACAROONS

**MAKES ABOUT
4 ½ DOZEN
COOKIES**

Coconut and almonds are a tempting combination, and here is a perfect example. Not only is the flavor unusual, the almond paste gives the cookies a unique texture.

5 CUPS SHREDDED UNSWEETENED
DRIED COCONUT

¼ CUP ALL-PURPOSE FLOUR

¼ TEASPOON SALT

2 ½ CUPS SUGAR

½ CUP (ABOUT 5 OUNCES) ALMOND
PASTE

8 LARGE EGG WHITES

1 TEASPOON PURE VANILLA EXTRACT

1. Position a rack in the middle of the oven and preheat the oven to 350°F. Line two large heavy baking sheets with silicone baking mats or parchment paper, or use two large nonstick baking sheets.

2. Stir together the coconut, flour, and salt with a fork in a medium bowl until well combined.

3. Using your hands, mix together the sugar and almond paste in a large deep heatproof bowl, breaking up the almond paste until the mixture resembles coarse meal. Add the egg whites and beat with an electric mixer on medium speed until smooth and well combined, scraping down the sides of the bowl as necessary. Beat in the vanilla.

4. Put the bowl over a large saucepan of about 1½ inches of barely simmering water, and heat, whisking constantly, for 5 minutes, or just until the mixture is too hot to touch. Remove the bowl from the heat, add the coconut mixture, and stir until well combined.

5. Drop the batter onto the baking sheets by generous tablespoons, spacing them about 1½ inches apart. Bake one sheet at a time, turning the baking sheet around halfway through, for about 20 minutes, or until golden brown. Let cool completely on the baking sheets on wire racks, then transfer to dry on the wire racks for about 1 hour. (The cookies can be stored in an airtight container at room temperature for up to 4 days.)

COCONUT MACAROONS WITH MACADAMIA NUTS

MAKES 3 ½ DOZEN COOKIES

Salted macadamia nuts are a very appealing counterpoint to sweet coconut. If you prefer, top only a half or a third of the cookies with the nuts.

3 LARGE EGG WHITES, AT ROOM TEMPERATURE

½ CUP SUGAR

¼ TEASPOON SALT

ONE 14-OUNCE PACKAGE (5 ¾ CUPS) SWEETENED FLAKED COCONUT

42 MACADAMIA NUTS

1. Position a rack in the middle of the oven and pre-heat the oven to 350°F. Line two large heavy baking sheets with silicone baking mats or parchment paper, or use two large nonstick baking sheets.

2. Whisk together the egg whites, sugar, and salt in a large bowl until frothy. With a fork, stir in the coconut until well combined.

3. Drop the batter by packed level tablespoons onto the baking sheets; the cookies can be placed close together because they will not spread. Smooth the cookies with damp fingers. Press a macadamia into the top of each one.

4. Bake one sheet at a time, turning the baking sheet around halfway through, for 25 to 30 minutes, until dark golden brown around the edges. Let cool completely on the baking sheets on wire racks. (The cookies can be stored in an airtight container at room temperature for up to 1 week.)

ELEGANT COCONUT AND CURRY BUTTER COOKIES

MAKES 3 DOZEN COOKIES

Curry powder in a cookie might seem odd, but it really works. The curry powder I use most often includes ground coriander, fenugreek, turmeric, cumin, black pepper, bay leaves, celery seed, nutmeg, cloves, onion, red pepper, and ginger. (For these cookies, I recommend a curry powder that doesn't contain garlic!)

1 ¼ CUPS ALL-PURPOSE FLOUR

1 CUP SWEETENED FLAKED COCONUT, TOASTED (SEE PAGE 10)

2 ½ TEASPOONS CURRY POWDER

¼ TEASPOON SALT

1 CUP (2 STICKS) UNSALTED BUTTER, AT ROOM TEMPERATURE

½ CUP SUGAR

¾ TEASPOON PURE COCONUT EXTRACT (SEE PAGE 17)

2 LARGE EGG YOLKS

1. Stir together the flour, toasted coconut, curry powder, and salt with a fork in a medium bowl.

2. Beat the butter, sugar, and coconut extract with an electric mixer in a large deep bowl, beginning on low speed and increasing to medium-high speed, until light and fluffy. Add the egg yolks and beat until well combined. Reduce the speed to low and add the flour mixture in two batches, beating just until blended. With a rubber spatula, stir in the coconut mixture.

3. If the dough is too soft, chill it for 1 hour, or until firm. Press the dough together with your hands and divide it in half. Place each half on a sheet of wax paper and form into a 7-by-1½-inch log. Smooth each log with damp fingers. Wrap the logs in wax paper and refrigerate for at least 2 hours, until thoroughly chilled and firm, or for up to 2 days.

4. Position a rack in the middle of the oven and pre-heat the oven to 400°F. Line two large heavy baking sheets with silicone baking mats or parchment paper, or use two large nonstick baking sheets.

5. With a sharp knife, cut each log crosswise into generous ¼-inch-thick rounds. Arrange the rounds 2 inches apart on the baking sheets.

6. Bake one sheet at a time, turning the baking sheet around halfway through, for 10 to 12 minutes, until the edges are golden brown. Let cool completely on the baking sheets on wire racks. (The cookies can be stored in an airtight container at room temperature for up to 3 days.)

DEEP DARK CHOCOLATE, COCONUT, AND GINGER BROWNIES

MAKES 2 DOZEN BROWNIES

It is easy to forget that chocolate is a tropical fruit, one of the reasons why it goes so well with coconut. Adding the ginger brings out the flavors even more.

1 CUP (2 STICKS) UNSALTED BUTTER, CUT INTO 8 PIECES

4 OUNCES UNSWEETENED CHOCOLATE, COARSELY CHOPPED

1½ CUPS SUGAR

5 LARGE EGGS

1 TEASPOON PURE VANILLA EXTRACT

¼ TEASPOON SALT

1 CUP ALL-PURPOSE FLOUR

¼ CUP UNSWEETENED COCOA POWDER

1½ CUPS SWEETENED FLAKED COCONUT, (1 CUP TOASTED, SEE PAGE 10)

2 TABLESPOONS FINELY CHOPPED CRYSTALLIZED GINGER

1. Position a rack in the middle of the oven and preheat the oven to 350°F. Lightly butter a 13-by-9-inch baking pan. Line the bottom with a piece of aluminum foil long enough to overhang the short sides by at least 2 inches, and butter the foil.

2. Melt the butter with the chocolate in a heatproof bowl set over a saucepan of about 1½ inches of barely simmering water, whisking until smooth. Remove the bowl from the heat and let cool.

3. Beat the sugar and eggs with an electric mixer on medium-high speed in a medium deep bowl until very thick and pale. Beat in the vanilla and salt. With a rubber spatula, fold in the chocolate mixture just until blended. Sift the flour and cocoa over the chocolate mixture and fold in just until blended. Fold in the toasted coconut and ginger.

4. Transfer the batter to the pan and smooth the top with a rubber spatula. Sprinkle evenly with the untoasted coconut. Bake for 25 to 30 minutes, until a toothpick inserted in the center comes out sticky with just a few crumbs but not wet; do not overbake. Let cool completely on a wire rack.

5. Lift up the edges of the foil, remove the brownies from the pan, and discard the foil. Cut the brownies lengthwise into 4 strips, then cut each strip crosswise into 6 bars. (The brownies can be stored in an airtight container at room temperature for up to 4 days.)

PUDDINGS AND OTHER SPOONABLE DESSERTS

The spoonable desserts here are very different from one another and varied in their country of origin.

The Creamy Coconut Bread Pudding (page 82) is boldly flavored with lemongrass and palm sugar. The "Put the Lime in the Coconut" Flan (page 84) is a true tropical treat, direct from the Caribbean. The individual servings of Coconut and Lemongrass Crème Caramel (page 86) are flavored with lemongrass, and with coconut rum, if you choose to use it. Brazilian in spirit, the big, beautiful Lighter-than-Air Coconut Jelly (page 89) is flavored with coconut milk, vanilla, and palm sugar, set with a bit of gelatin, and lightened with beaten egg whites. The texture is fantastic, and it is a showpiece dessert. I am very fond of the Young Coconut Water and Coconut Milk Jelly (page 92). You just mix the coconut milk and coconut water with gelatin and sugar and then, as it chills, it separates naturally into a thick rich coconut milk layer and a layer of opalescent young coconut water jelly. When you invert it onto a plate for serving, it is beautiful, and it has two very different, pleasing textures. There is also a Thai-style tapioca pudding. The Samui Island Bananas (page 93), made with coconut milk and bananas, is very smooth and satisfying and very coconutty.

CREAMY COCONUT BREAD PUDDING

SERVES 6 TO 8

This is quintessential comfort food, which is most often all about texture, and here the coconut flavor adds to the coziness. There are several textures going on that play very well together: the ultrarich custard and the silky-soft bread are variations on smooth and creamy, and together they are a perfect foil for the crisp, crackly, toasty coconut. This is lovely just as it is, but you might serve Bananas Foster (page 102) or Caramelized Pineapple (page 141) on the side, or use Candied Coconut (page 141) or crushed Coconut Praline (page 138) as a garnish. If you'd like, steep an aromatic pandan leaf (see page 20) in the half-and-half with the coconut for even better, more complex flavor and aroma.

6 CUPS ½-INCH CUBES WHITE BREAD (WITH CRUST)

2 CUPS HALF-AND-HALF

1 ½ CUPS SHREDDED UNSWEETENED DRIED COCONUT, TOASTED (SEE PAGE 10)

ONE 13 ½- OR 14-OUNCE CAN UNSWEETENED COCONUT MILK

2 STALKS LEMONGRASS, TRIMMED AND THINLY SLICED

PINCH OF SALT

6 LARGE EGGS

⅓ CUP SHAVED PALM SUGAR OR PACKED LIGHT BROWN SUGAR

1. Preheat the oven to 350°F. Butter an 8-inch square glass baking dish.

2. Spread the bread cubes on a large heavy baking sheet and toast in the oven, stirring once, for 15 minutes, or until pale golden brown. Transfer to a plate.

3. Bring the half-and-half, 1 cup of the toasted coconut, the coconut milk, the lemongrass, and salt to a full boil in a large heavy saucepan over medium-high heat. Remove the pan from the heat, cover, and let steep for 30 minutes.

4. Pour the half-and-half mixture through a fine-mesh strainer set over a large glass measure or bowl, pressing hard on the solids to extract as much liquid as possible. Set the saucepan aside.

5. Whisk together the eggs and sugar in a large bowl. Slowly pour in the half-and-half mixture, whisking constantly. Return the mixture to the saucepan and cook, whisking constantly, over medium-low heat for 5 to 7 minutes, until the custard has thickened and coats the back of a spoon; if you draw your finger across it, it should leave a track. Do not let

the custard boil or scorch; if tiny bubbles appear around the edges, remove the pan from the heat for a few minutes to cool the custard, continuing to whisk. Pour the custard through a large fine-mesh strainer set over a large glass measure or bowl.

6. Put the toasted bread in the prepared baking dish. Pour the custard over it and push the bread down with a spoon to submerge it. Let stand for 30 minutes, or until the bread is softened.

7. Meanwhile, preheat the oven to 300°F. Have a large baking pan ready. Put on a kettle of water to boil for a water bath.

8. Cover the baking dish with aluminum foil and seal the edges tightly. Put the baking dish in the baking pan, place in the oven, and carefully pour enough boiling water into the roasting pan to come halfway up the sides of the baking dish. Bake for 1 hour.

9. Remove the foil and bake the bread pudding for 15 minutes longer, or until the top is pale golden brown but the center is still slightly jiggly. Carefully remove the baking dish from the pan and let cool slightly on a wire rack.

10. Spoon the warm pudding into bowls and sprinkle with the remaining toasted coconut. Serve immediately.

"PUT THE LIME IN THE COCONUT" FLAN

SERVES 10

A flan flavored with lime and coconut is a fine tropical pleasure, so fine you may find yourself singing the old calypso tune. Nothing disappoints me more than a flan without enough caramel—you won't have that problem with this one! The flan is wonderful just as it is, but you could serve it with fresh cherries and raspberries or sliced peaches and strawberries.

2 ¼ CUPS HALF-AND-HALF

1 CUP SHREDDED UNSWEETENED DRIED COCONUT, TOASTED (SEE PAGE 10)

2 TEASPOONS FINELY GRATED LIME ZEST

1 ¾ CUPS SUGAR

¼ CUP WATER

6 LARGE EGGS

3 LARGE EGG YOLKS

PINCH OF SALT

1. Preheat the oven to 325°F. Have a 9-by-1½-inch round cake pan and a large baking pan ready.

2. Bring the half-and-half, toasted coconut, and lime zest to a full boil in a large heavy saucepan over medium-high heat. Remove the pan from the heat, cover, and let steep for 25 minutes.

3. Meanwhile, heat 1 cup of the sugar and the water in a medium heavy saucepan over medium heat, stirring, until the sugar is dissolved. Increase the heat to high and bring the mixture to a boil, wash-ing down the sides of the pan with a wet pastry brush if you see any sugar crystals. Boil, without stirring, swirling the pan toward the end to even out the color, until the caramel is a dark amber. Immediately pour the caramel into the cake pan, tilting to coat the bottom evenly. Let cool and harden at room temperature.

4. Put on a kettle of water to boil for a water bath. Pour the half-and-half mixture into a medium glass measure.

5. Whisk together the eggs, yolks, remaining ¾ cup sugar, and the salt in a large deep bowl until well combined. Slowly pour in the half-and-half mixture, whisking constantly, until blended and smooth. Pour the mixture through a fine-mesh

strainer set over a large glass measure or bowl with a spout, pressing hard on the solids to extract as much liquid as possible.

6. Pour the custard into the caramel-lined pan. Put the cake pan in the large baking pan, place it in the oven, and carefully pour enough boiling water into the baking pan to reach halfway up the sides of the cake pan. Bake for 35 to 40 minutes, until the custard is set around the edges but still slightly jiggly in the center; do not overbake—the custard will set further as it cools.

7. Remove the cake pan from the water bath and let cool to room temperature on a wire rack. Refrigerate, loosely covered, for about 6 hours, until thoroughly chilled and set, or for up to 1 day.

8. Run a table knife around the edge of the cake pan to loosen the custard. Invert the flan onto a serving platter and serve cut into wedges.

COCONUT AND LEMONGRASS CRÈME CARAMEL

SERVES 4

I've said it before, and I'll say it again, crème caramel is my all-time favorite dessert. And this one, flavored with both coconut and lemongrass, may be my most beloved. You don't have to add the coconut rum, but it will add more coconut flavor as well as warmth. Add a pandan leaf (see page 20), an aromatic known as the vanilla of Asia, if you have one, to the saucepan when you steep the coconut and lemongrass. You will be very pleased with the flavor.

1 ¼ CUPS HALF-AND-HALF

1 CUP SWEETENED FLAKED COCONUT, TOASTED (SEE PAGE 10)

1 STALK LEMONGRASS, TRIMMED AND THINLY SLICED

½ CUP SUGAR

¼ CUP WATER

4 LARGE EGG YOLKS

PINCH OF SALT

1 TABLESPOON COCONUT RUM, PREFERABLY MALIBU (OPTIONAL)

1. Preheat the oven to 325°F. Have four 6-ounce rame-kins or custard cups and a large baking pan ready.

2. Bring the half-and-half, toasted coconut, and lemon-grass to a full boil in a medium heavy saucepan over medium-high heat. Remove the pan from the heat, cover, and let steep for 25 minutes.

3. Meanwhile, heat the sugar and water in a medium heavy saucepan over medium heat, stirring, until the sugar is dissolved. Increase the heat to high and bring the mixture to a boil, washing down the sides of the pan with a wet pastry brush if you see any sugar crystals. Boil, without stirring, swirling the pan toward the end to even out the color, until the caramel is a dark amber. Immediately pour the caramel into the ramekins, tilting to coat the bottom and sides evenly (you may have some left over). Let cool and harden at room temperature.

4. Put on a kettle of water to boil for a water bath. Whisk together the egg yolks and salt in a medium bowl. Slowly pour in the half-and-half mixture, whisking constantly. Pour the custard through a fine-mesh strainer set over a medium glass mea-sure or a bowl with a spout, pressing hard on the solids to extract as much liquid as possible. Whisk in the coconut rum (if using).

Continued

5. Divide the custard evenly among the ramekins. Put the ramekins in the baking pan, place it in the oven, and carefully pour enough boiling water into the pan to reach halfway up the sides of the ramekins. Bake for 30 to 35 minutes, until the custard is set around the edges but the center is still slightly jiggly; do not overbake—the custards will set further as they cool.

6. With tongs or a wide metal spatula, carefully transfer the ramekins to a wire rack, and let cool to room temperature. Refrigerate, tightly covered, for at least 3 hours, until thoroughly chilled and set, or for up to 1 day.

7. Run a table knife around the edges of the ramekins and invert onto chilled serving plates.

LIGHTER-THAN-AIR COCONUT JELLY

SERVES 8

This luscious coconut jelly is adapted from a recipe sent to *Gourmet* magazine by a reader, Maria Pereira. It has a fantastic texture and flavor and is a real crowd-pleaser. If you have one, use a decorative 9- to 12-cup mold instead of a Bundt pan. The jelly is terrific served with fresh fruit—try apricots and raspberries, mango and blackberries, or nectarines and blueberries. For maximum impact, make sure everyone sees the whole dessert before you cut it into servings.

½ CUP WHOLE MILK

TWO ¼-OUNCE ENVELOPES GELATIN

2 CUPS HALF-AND-HALF

1 CUP GRANULATED SUGAR

½ CUP SHAVED PALM SUGAR OR PACKED LIGHT BROWN SUGAR

¼ TEASPOON SALT

ONE 13½- OR 14-OUNCE CAN UNSWEETENED COCONUT MILK

½ TEASPOON PURE VANILLA EXTRACT

4 LARGE EGG WHITES, AT ROOM TEMPERATURE

1. Pour the milk into a small heatproof bowl, sprinkle the gelatin over it, and let stand for about 5 minutes, or until softened. Put the bowl in a larger bowl of hot water and stir until the gelatin has dissolved.

2. Bring the half-and-half, ½ cup of the granulated sugar, the palm sugar, and salt to a boil in a medium saucepan over medium-high heat, whisking until the sugar is dissolved. Remove the pan from the heat and whisk in the gelatin mixture. Pour the mixture through a fine-mesh strainer set over a large bowl, then whisk in the coconut milk and vanilla until smooth. Let cool to room temperature, whisking occasionally (this will take about 45 minutes).

3. Lightly oil a 10-cup Bundt pan. Beat the egg whites with an electric mixer on medium-high speed in a large deep bowl just until they hold soft peaks when the beaters are lifted. Gradually beat in the remaining ½ cup granulated sugar, about 1 tablespoon at a time, and beat just until the whites hold stiff peaks when the beaters are lifted.

4. With a whisk or a rubber spatula, fold one-third of the egg whites into the coconut milk mixture to lighten it, then fold in the remaining egg whites.

Continued

5. Pour the mixture into the Bundt pan. Refrigerate, uncovered, for about 6 hours, until thoroughly chilled and set, or for up to 1 day.

6. Gently run a rubber spatula around the edge of the Bundt pan. Fill a large bowl with very warm water, dip the bottom of the pan into the water for about 15 seconds, and invert the jelly onto a serving platter; carefully lift off the pan. Cut into slices and serve on chilled plates.

YOUNG COCONUT WATER AND COCONUT MILK JELLY

SERVES 6

This unusual dessert separates beautifully on standing. It's a perfect way to see and enjoy the differences between young coconut water and coconut milk—think of it as a dessert "science project." Because it is so simple, you need to use the best ingredients possible. That means young coconut water with no additives or pulp and the best coconut milk you can get your hands on. Consider making your own coconut milk for this dish, or use a very good canned one from Thailand (see page 12). I love this jelly garnished with sliced lychees, either canned or fresh, tossed with fresh raspberries. It's also great garnished with Candied Coconut (page 141) or crushed Coconut Praline (page 138). This is actually a very easy, very quick dessert, and will be a real treat for your guests.

1 CUP FRESH OR ASEPTIC-PACKAGED 100% YOUNG COCONUT WATER

1 TABLESPOON GELATIN

2 CUPS FRESH OR WELL-STIRRED CANNED UNSWEETENED COCONUT MILK

¼ CUP SUGAR

PINCH OF SALT

1. Lightly oil six 6-ounce ramekins or custard cups.

2. Pour ¼ cup of the coconut water into a small heatproof bowl, sprinkle the gelatin over it, and let stand for about 5 minutes, or until softened. Put the bowl in a larger bowl of hot water and stir until the gelatin has dissolved.

3. Bring the remaining coconut water, the coconut milk, sugar, and salt just to a boil in a large heavy saucepan over medium-high heat, stirring until the sugar is dissolved. Remove the pan from the heat and whisk in the gelatin mixture. Pour the mixture through a fine-mesh strainer set over a medium glass measure or a bowl with a spout.

4. Divide the mixture evenly among the ramekins and let cool to room temperature. Refrigerate the jelly, loosely covered, for at least 3 hours, until thoroughly chilled and set, or for up to 1 day.

5. Dip the bottoms of the ramekins, one at a time, into a bowl of hot water for about 5 seconds, then run a table knife around the edges of the jellies and invert onto chilled serving plates.

SAMUI ISLAND BANANAS

SERVES 4

Koh Samui is a gorgeous island in the Gulf of Thailand, and it is a true tropical paradise. It has gorgeous beaches with tall, swaying coconut palms, and it is said to export more than a million coconuts a month. In the not-so-distant past, many were harvested by monkeys, who could each pick up to a thousand coconuts a day! So, as you might imagine, they use a lot of coconuts in the cuisine of the island. This is a memorable dessert I enjoyed there. In Thailand, they might add half a teaspoon or so of rose water or a drop or two of jasmine essence to this dish, and so could you, if you'd like. In Southeast Asia, they would use honey or ladies' finger bananas; here you could use tiny Mexican bananas if you can get them. Instead of the sesame seeds, you might garnish the dish with just a sprinkle of Toasted Coconut Sugar (page 135).

---

1 ½ TEASPOONS SESAME SEEDS

1 ½ CUPS FRESH OR WELL-STIRRED CANNED UNSWEETENED COCONUT MILK

¾ CUP WATER

½ CUP SUGAR

¼ CUP SMALL TAPIOCA PEARLS (NOT INSTANT TAPIOCA)

LARGE PINCH OF SALT

2 FIRM BUT RIPE MEDIUM BANANAS, PEELED, STRINGS DISCARDED, AND CUT CROSSWISE INTO QUARTERS

1. Toast the sesame seeds in a small skillet over medium heat, stirring constantly, for 3 to 5 minutes, until golden brown and fragrant. Transfer to a saucer to cool.

2. Bring the coconut milk and water just to a boil in a large heavy saucepan over medium heat. Stir in the sugar, tapioca, and salt, reduce the heat, and cook at a low simmer, stirring occasionally to prevent sticking, for about 15 minutes, until the tapioca is soft and translucent.

3. Stir in the bananas, return to a simmer, and simmer for about 5 minutes, until the bananas are slightly softened.

4. Divide the mixture evenly among serving bowls. Serve hot or warm, topped with the sesame seeds.

SPECIAL FAVORITES

Here's a selection of
exceptional desserts
with inspirations
from around the world.

Take baklava—the queen of sweets from the
Middle East and Europe is wonderful made
with coconut. And Coconut and Pistachio
Baklava (page 96), flavored with fresh lime
and orange flower water, is unique and delicious, a very special treat. Pavlova is a big
meringue topped with whipped cream and
fruit. Here you'll find Luscious Coconut
and Mango Pavlova (page 110), a coconut
meringue topped with a coconut and mango
curd whipped with cream. It has an intense
mango and coconut flavor and is gorgeous.
An all-American shortcake, Bananas Foster
Shortcake with Coconut Biscuits (page 102),
is made with a coconut biscuit and the classic New Orleans treat, Bananas Foster. The
Coconut and Raspberry Cream Puff Gâteau
(page 99)—an elegant "layer cake" made with
pâte a choux (cream puff) dough from clas-
sical French cuisine—is layered with cream,
raspberry sauce, and candied coconut.

The Coconut-Fried Bananas (page 105) are
great with ice cream. Matrimony (page 106),
from the Caribbean, is perfectly simple—
sliced oranges and ribbons of fresh coconut
seasoned with a bit of sugar, allspice, and
a pinch of salt. It's an appropriate dessert
anytime. It's likely that few of your friends
or family have seen South African baby
pineapples and the Caramel-and-Coconut-
Coated Baby Pineapples (page 112) will be a
unique and delicious treat for them. When
you've got your grill going, consider tossing
together the Grilled Pineapple Satays with
Coconut Dulce de Leche (page 111). Classic
Eton mess is prepared with strawberries, but
Tropical Eton Mess (page 109) is made with
the same coconut meringue as the Pavlova,
crumbled, mixed with heavy cream, and
topped with sweetened ripe mangoes tossed
with lime.

COCONUT AND PISTACHIO BAKLAVA

MAKES 24 PIECES

I use a French orange flower water, Vallauris brand, that I brought back from Nice. If your orange flower water is from the Middle East (most often Lebanon) you will need to use more to taste; the Middle Eastern–style is not as strongly flavored as the French version. I also use Athens brand phyllo (it says "fillo" on the box), which comes in a 1-pound container with two separate packages inside. Make sure to use unsalted pistachios. This baklava is actually not at all difficult to make, but take care not to press down on the layers of pastry as you layer and then cut them.

ONE 1-POUND BOX PHYLLO DOUGH (SEE HEADNOTE), THAWED IF FROZEN

1 ¼ CUPS (2 ½ STICKS) UNSALTED BUTTER, MELTED

FILLING

2 ½ CUPS SHREDDED UNSWEETENED DRIED COCONUT

¾ CUP COARSELY CHOPPED UNSALTED PISTACHIOS

½ CUP SUGAR

¼ CUP WATER

1 TABLESPOON ORANGE FLOWER WATER

PINCH OF SALT

Continued

1. Preheat the oven to 350°F. Butter a 13-by-9-by-2-inch baking pan.

2. Unfold the sheets of phyllo dough, lay the stack on a work surface, and cover with wax paper and then a damp kitchen towel to keep it from drying out. Remove 2 pieces of phyllo, place them in the pan, and brush them with 1 tablespoon of the butter. Continue in the same way with the phyllo and butter until you have used 24 sheets of phyllo.

3. To make the filling: Stir together the coconut, pistachios, sugar, water, orange flower water, and salt in a medium bowl. Sprinkle half of the filling evenly over the phyllo in the pan. Place 2 sheets of phyllo in the pan and brush them with 1 tablespoon butter. Continue in the same way until you have used 12 sheets of phyllo. Spread the remaining filling on top. Layer and butter the remaining phyllo in the same way. Brush the top layer of pastry generously with butter, and pour any remaining butter over the top. With a sharp knife, cut the baklava lengthwise into 4 strips and then crosswise into 6 strips, taking care not to press down on the phyllo.

4. Bake for 30 minutes. Lower the oven temperature to 300°F and bake for 1 hour and 10 to 15 minutes, until golden brown.

Continued

SYRUP

1 ¾ CUPS SUGAR

1 ½ CUPS WATER

LARGE PINCH OF SALT

3 TABLESPOONS ORANGE FLOWER
WATER

3 TABLESPOONS FRESH LIME JUICE

2 TABLESPOONS FINELY CHOPPED
UNSALTED PISTACHIOS

5. To make the syrup: Bring the sugar, water, and salt to a boil in a medium saucepan over medium-high heat, stirring until the sugar is dissolved. Reduce the heat and simmer for 10 minutes, or until slightly thickened. Remove the saucepan from the heat and stir in the orange flower water and lime juice.

6. Transfer the baklava to a wire rack and let cool for 10 minutes. Sprinkle with the chopped pistachios and pour the syrup evenly over the top. Let cool completely on the rack. (The baklava can be stored at room temperature, tightly covered, for up to 2 days.)

7. Cut into pieces with a sharp knife and serve.

COCONUT AND RASPBERRY CREAM PUFF GÂTEAU

SERVES 8

I recommend a stand mixer for this recipe, because of the length of time it takes to beat the pastry dough as it cools to room temperature. The raspberries, coconut, and cream are a lovely combination, and if it appeals to you, add about half a cup of finely diced ripe mango with the raspberries between the layers. This has the look of something that is difficult to make, but it's not.

PASTRY

1 CUP WATER

½ CUP (1 STICK) UNSALTED BUTTER, CUT INTO ½-INCH PIECES

2 TABLESPOONS SUGAR

¼ TEASPOON SALT

1 ½ CUPS ALL-PURPOSE FLOUR

5 LARGE EGGS, AT ROOM TEMPERATURE

SAUCE

3 CUPS FRESH OR THAWED FROZEN RASPBERRIES

½ TO ¾ CUP CONFECTIONERS' SUGAR, DEPENDING ON THE SWEETNESS OF THE BERRIES

¼ CUP WATER

PINCH OF SALT

1 TO 2 TEASPOONS FRESH LEMON JUICE

Continued

1. To make the pastry: Position a rack in the middle of the oven and preheat the oven to 400°F. Generously butter and flour three 9-by-1 ½-inch round cake pans.

2. Bring the water, butter, sugar, and salt to a boil in a large heavy saucepan over high heat, stirring until the butter is melted. Remove the pan from the heat, add the flour all at once, and stir vigorously with a wooden spoon until the mixture pulls away from the sides of the pan, forming a ball. Transfer the mixture to a large deep bowl (preferably the bowl of a stand mixer) and, with an electric mixer on high speed, add the eggs one at a time, beating well after each addition and scraping down the sides of the bowl as necessary. Continue beating until the mixture is smooth and dry looking and has cooled to room temperature.

3. Divide the batter evenly among the cake pans and spread it evenly with a small offset spatula.

4. Bake the pastry for 20 minutes. Lower the oven temperature to 350°F and bake for 15 minutes longer, or until dark golden brown, puffed, and crisp. Let cool in the pans on wire racks for 5 minutes (the layers will fall). Run a table knife around the sides of the pans, turn the layers out of the pans, and cool completely, right-side up, on the racks.

Continued

1 ½ CUPS HEAVY (WHIPPING) CREAM

3 TABLESPOONS OF CONFECTIONERS' SUGAR

1 CUP FRESH RASPBERRIES

1 ¼ CUPS CANDIED COCONUT (PAGE 141)

5. To make the sauce: Pulse the berries in a food processor just until broken up. Sift the ½ to ¾ cup confectioners' sugar over the berries, add the water and salt, and pulse once or twice. Add lemon juice to taste. Pour the mixture through a large coarse-mesh strainer set over a bowl, pressing hard on the solids to extract as much liquid as possible.Let cool to room temperature. (The sauce can be refrigerated, tightly covered, for up to 2 weeks. Shake or stir well before serving. The sauce will thicken a bit on standing; add water as needed to thin to the desired consistency.)

6. Beat the cream with an electric mixer on medium-high speed in a large deep bowl until the cream holds soft peaks when the beaters are lifted. Add the 3 tablespoons confectioners' sugar and beat until the cream forms stiff peaks when the beaters are lifted.

7. Place one pastry layer on a serving plate. Spread with one-third of the whipped cream, top with ⅓ cup of the raspberry sauce, sprinkle with ⅓ cup of the raspberries, and top with ¼ cup of the candied coconut. Repeat with the remaining two pastry layers, sprinkling the top with the remaining ¼ cup candied coconut. (Reserve the remaining raspberry sauce for another use.) Cut into wedges with a sharp serrated knife and serve with knives and forks.

BANANAS FOSTER SHORTCAKE WITH COCONUT BISCUITS

SERVES 4

One of the great dishes of American cuisine, bananas Foster comes from Brennan's restaurant in New Orleans, where it's served as a finale to their famous brunch. The sweet, buttery, warm bananas are wonderful served on their own. The idea to serve it with a coconut-flavored shortcake biscuit is mine—and I hope you will like it as much as I do. Be careful not to overcook the bananas; you want them to be just softened and still holding their shape. Banana liqueur is traditional, but I prefer coconut rum here. Use slightly sweetened whipped cream instead of the ice cream, if you like.

SHORTCAKES

1 ½ CUPS ALL-PURPOSE FLOUR

½ CUP SWEETENED FLAKED COCONUT, TOASTED (SEE PAGE 10)

¼ CUP SUGAR

1 TABLESPOON BAKING POWDER

PINCH OF SALT

6 TABLESPOONS (¾ STICK) COLD UNSALTED BUTTER, CUT INTO SMALL PIECES

¼ CUP WHOLE MILK

BANANAS FOSTER

3 MEDIUM BANANAS

¼ CUP (½ STICK) UNSALTED BUTTER

½ CUP PACKED LIGHT BROWN SUGAR

1 TEASPOON FRESH LEMON JUICE

PINCH OF SALT

2 TABLESPOONS COCONUT RUM, PREFERABLY MALIBU (OPTIONAL)

1. To make the shortcakes: Preheat the oven to 450°F.

2. Butter a baking sheet. Whisk together the flour, toasted coconut, sugar, baking powder, and salt in a medium bowl. Cut in the butter with a pastry blender or two knives used scissors-fashion until the mixture resembles coarse crumbs. Pour in the milk and stir with a fork just until blended.

3. Turn the dough out onto a lightly floured surface and knead a couple of times. Transfer to a lightly floured sheet of wax paper and pat out to about ½ inch thick. Using a 3½-inch cutter, cut out four rounds (gather the scraps together, pat out again, and cut out more biscuits as necessary). Transfer the biscuits to the baking sheet.

4. Bake for about 15 minutes, until pale golden brown.

5. To make the bananas Foster: Peel the bananas and discard the strings. Cut each crosswise in half and then lengthwise in half. Heat the butter, brown sugar, lemon juice, and salt in a large nonstick skillet over medium heat, stirring, until the sugar is melted. Add the bananas, and cook, shaking the pan and gently turning the bananas, for 2 minutes,

TOASTED COCONUT ICE CREAM (PAGE 124), COCONUT AND FRESH GINGER ICE CREAM (PAGE 122), OR YOUR FAVORITE ICE CREAM

or just until they are beginning to soften. If you would like to flambé the bananas, add the coconut rum and heat the mixture, then carefully tip the pan slightly to ignite the rum, or light it with a long match.

6. Place each biscuit on a serving plate. Spoon the bananas next to the biscuits, and add a scoop of ice cream to each plate. Serve immediately.

COCONUT-FRIED BANANAS

SERVES 4

In Indonesia, fried bananas are called *pisang goring*. They make a fine break-fast and are especially good when served with Balinese or Sumatran coffee. We're more likely to enjoy this as dessert, and it is wonderful with ice cream, especially Toasted Coconut Ice Cream (page 124). The bananas really are best served immediately, in batches, as they are pulled from the pan; people don't mind waiting a bit for food at its best. If you don't want to serve them as they are done, preheat the oven to 250°F, drain the bananas on paper towels, and keep them warm in the oven on a baking sheet lined with paper towels.

VEGETABLE OIL FOR DEEP-FRYING

1 ½ CUPS ALL-PURPOSE FLOUR

3 TABLESPOONS SUGAR

¾ TEASPOON BAKING SODA

PINCH OF SALT

1 CUP WATER

1 LARGE EGG

1 LARGE EGG YOLK

6 TABLESPOONS SHREDDED UNSWEET-ENED DRIED COCONUT

4 FIRM BUT RIPE BANANAS

1. Heat about 2 inches of oil to 375°F in a large heavy saucepan over medium-high heat. Place several layers of paper towels on a large baking sheet.

2. Meanwhile, whisk together the flour, sugar, baking soda, and salt in a large bowl. Whisk together the water, egg, and egg yolk in a medium glass measure. Pour the egg mixture into the dry ingredients and whisk together to make a thin batter. Whisk in the coconut until well combined.

3. Peel the bananas, discard the strings, cut the bananas crosswise into quarters, and cut each piece lengthwise in half. Dip 4 to 6 banana pieces into the batter at a time, then shake off the excess, and gently drop into the oil, keeping the pieces separate. Deep-fry, turning occasionally, for about 2 minutes for each batch, until deep golden brown. Remove the bananas with a slotted spoon and drain on the paper towels. Serve hot.

MATRIMONY

The classic West Indian combination of oranges and coconut is so perfect a marriage it earned the name "matrimony." When I was about five years old, I thought the ambrosia my mom made was about the most exotic food on Earth. Now I realize what those canned mandarin oranges and packaged sweetened coconut meant to be was this. My mom would have loved it. It looks gorgeous on a glass platter.

4 LARGE NAVEL ORANGES

1 TABLESPOON SUGAR

SCANT ¼ TEASPOON GROUND ALLSPICE

PINCH OF SALT

½ CUP FRESH COCONUT RIBBONS
(SEE PAGE 10)

1. With a sharp knife, remove the tops and bottoms of the oranges. Following the shapes of the oranges, remove the peel and white pith in wide strips from top to bottom. Cut the oranges crosswise into slices about ⅜ inch thick. Discard any seeds. Arrange the slices in overlapping circles on a platter.

2. Stir together the sugar, allspice, and salt in a small bowl and sprinkle over the oranges. Top with the coconut. Refrigerate, tightly covered, for 1 to 2 hours, until very cold.

3. Serve chilled, spooning any juice released by the oranges over the oranges and coconut.

TROPICAL ETON MESS

SERVES 6 TO 8

The traditional Eton Mess is prepared with glorious English strawberries and that incredible English cream, mashed together with crumbled meringue. It may be a mess, but it is delicious. This tropical version made with mangoes and coconut meringue is just as lush and has the same fabulous textures.

2 TEASPOONS FINELY GRATED LIME ZEST

¼ CUP FRESH LIME JUICE

PINCH OF SALT

3 RIPE MANGOES, PEELED, SEEDED, AND CUT INTO ½-INCH DICE

1 CUP HEAVY (WHIPPING) CREAM

MERINGUE FROM LUSCIOUS COCONUT AND MANGO PAVLOVA (PAGE 110), BROKEN INTO APPROXIMATELY 1 ½-INCH PIECES

CANDIED COCONUT, FOR GARNISH (PAGE 141; OPTIONAL)

1. Stir together the lime zest, lime juice, and salt in a medium bowl. Gently stir in the mangoes.

2. Beat the cream with an electric mixer on medium-high speed in a large deep bowl until the cream holds soft peaks when the beaters are lifted.

3. Stir together the meringue and whipped cream in a serving bowl. Spoon the mango mixture over the cream mixture. Top with the candied coconut, if desired. Serve immediately.

LUSCIOUS COCONUT AND MANGO PAVLOVA

SERVES 8

Pavlova is the national dessert of Australia. Instead of the toasted coconut, you might use Candied Coconut (page 141) or Toasted Coconut Sugar (page 135) for garnish. Make sure the curd is well chilled before assembling the dessert. If the weather is hot, you might want to chill the curd and cream mixture for a few minutes before filling the meringue basket.

4 LARGE EGG WHITES, AT ROOM TEMPERATURE

¼ TEASPOON CREAM OF TARTAR

PINCH OF SALT

¾ CUP SUGAR

¾ CUP PLUS 2 TABLESPOONS SWEETENED FLAKED COCONUT, TOASTED (SEE PAGE 10)

¾ CUP HEAVY (WHIPPING) CREAM

LUSCIOUS COCONUT AND MANGO CURD (PAGE 134)

1. Position a rack in the middle of the oven and pre-heat the oven to 225°F. Trace a 9-inch circle on parchment paper and put on a baking sheet.

2. Beat the egg whites with an electric mixer on medium speed in a large bowl until foamy. Increase the speed to medium-high, add the cream of tartar and salt, and beat just until the egg whites hold soft peaks when the beaters are lifted. Gradually add the sugar, about 1 tablespoon at a time, and continue beating just until the whites hold stiff peaks. With a rubber spatula, fold in ¾ cup of the toasted coconut.

3. Spoon the meringue into the traced circle, scooping the sides upward to form a nest. Bake for 1 hour, or until the meringue is dry to the touch. Turn off the oven and leave the meringue in the oven for 2 hours.

4. Just before serving, beat the cream with an electric mixer on medium-high speed in a medium deep bowl just until it holds stiff peaks when the beaters are lifted. Beat in the curd just until well combined. Peel off the paper from the meringue. Spoon the filling into the meringue shell and sprinkle the remaining toasted coconut on top. Serve immediately.

GRILLED PINEAPPLE SATAYS WITH COCONUT DULCE DE LECHE

SERVES 8

There's something wonderful about fruit on a stick, especially when you can dip it into something sweet and coconutty. Feel free to serve ice cream or sorbet on the side of this dish—try the Piña Colada Sorbet on page 117.

1 RIPE SMALL PINEAPPLE, PEELED AND EYES REMOVED (SEE PAGE 22)

COCONUT DULCE DE LECHE (PAGE 132), AT ROOM TEMPERATURE

1. Soak sixteen 12-inch-long bamboo skewers in water for 30 minutes. Prepare a medium-high fire in a charcoal or gas grill.

2. Meanwhile, cut the pineapple lengthwise into quarters and remove the core. Cut each quarter into four lengthwise slices. Thread each wedge lengthwise onto a skewer. Put the dulce de leche in a small serving bowl.

3. Grill the pineapple, turning, for about 5 minutes, until softened and well marked. Transfer the skewers to a serving platter and serve with the dulce de leche for dipping.

CARAMEL-AND-COCONUT-COATED BABY PINEAPPLES

SERVES 4

Also known as Queen Victoria pineapples, baby pineapples come from South Africa and are sweet and tart as all good pineapples are, with a bold, rich flavor. They are entirely edible; there is no need to remove the core. Look for baby pineapples that are brightly colored and have deep green leaves. They weigh about 8 ounces each, are about 2 inches wide, and, with the leaves, they measure only about 4 ½ inches tall.

They are wonderful (as long as you're careful not to cut your fingers on the very sharp tiny stickers on the leaves), and one of the great things about them is they are a perfect size for a single serving. If your supermarket doesn't carry them, try www.melissas.com. The caramel will firm up quickly, so have everything all ready before coating all the pineapples with the caramel and the coconut.

---

4 RIPE SOUTH AFRICAN BABY PINEAPPLES, LEAVES LEFT ATTACHED, PEEL AND EYES REMOVED (SEE PAGE 22)

¾ CUP SWEETENED FLAKED COCONUT

1 CUP SUGAR

¼ CUP FRESH LIME JUICE

3 TABLESPOONS WATER

1 TABLESPOON MINCED FRESH GINGER

PINCH OF SALT

1. Have a baking sheet with a rim ready. Dry the pineapples with a clean kitchen towel. Put the coconut on a plate.

2. Heat the sugar, lime juice, water, ginger, and salt in a medium heavy saucepan over medium heat, stirring, until the sugar is dissolved. Increase the heat to high and bring the mixture to a boil, washing down the sides of the pan with a wet pastry brush if you see any sugar crystals. Boil, without stirring, swirling the pan toward the end to even out the color, until the caramel is a pale gold.

3. Immediately pour the hot caramel onto one end of the baking sheet. Quickly roll the pineapples, one at a time, in the caramel to coat evenly, then roll in the coconut to coat evenly. Stand the pineapples up on a platter.

4. Serve immediately, or let stand at room temperature, loosely covered, for up to 3 hours.

FROZEN DESSERTS

Here is a selection of thoroughly tropical sorbets, along with ice creams, a granita, a ginger beer ice cream float, and "snowballs."

The Toasted Coconut Ice Cream (page 124) is the essence of toasted coconut and custard. The Coconut and Fresh Ginger Ice Cream (page 122) is just as rich and creamy, with the additional intense flavor and warmth of fresh ginger. Both say coconut in a loud voice— they do not whisper. All of the sorbets are very easy to make, but each one highlights an extraordinary coconut flavor combination: coconut and mango, coconut and lychee, and coconut and pineapple. I don't think there is a dessert more refreshing than the Coconut and Lemongrass Granita (page 121). You will also find Toasted Snowballs with Coconut Chocolate Sauce (page 125), ice-cream balls rolled in toasted coconut and served in a pool of coconut-flavored chocolate sauce.

And, finally, there's a Ginger Beer Ice Cream Float (page 126), made with ginger beer and coconut ice cream.

QUICK CHILL

Instead of waiting for hours for the mixtures in these recipes to chill, try the quick-chill method: Pour the ice cream or other mixture into a large glass measure or a deep bowl and put it in a shorter large bowl. Add ice and water to the large bowl and stir or whisk the ice cream mixture occasionally, adding more ice to the water as it melts, until chilled. (Make sure no ice gets in the mixture.) As an alternative, you can put the mixture in a self-sealing plastic bag and submerge it in the ice water until it is cold.

PIÑA COLADA SORBET

**SERVES 4 TO 6
(MAKES 5 CUPS)**

I use the pineapple juice that comes in glass jars; it doesn't taste like the can and has better color. This is delightful topped with toasted unsweetened coconut, either fresh or dried. Or with Coconut Tuiles (page 69) on the side, or Coconut-Caramel Popcorn (page 139) sprinkled on top.

1 ¾ CUPS FRESH OR WELL-STIRRED
CANNED UNSWEETENED COCONUT MILK

1 CUP SHAVED PALM SUGAR OR PACKED
LIGHT BROWN SUGAR

PINCH OF SALT

2 CUPS CHILLED PINEAPPLE JUICE

3 TABLESPOONS FRESH LIME JUICE

1 TABLESPOON COCONUT RUM,
PREFERABLY MALIBU (OPTIONAL)

1. Bring the coconut milk, sugar, and salt just to a boil in a medium saucepan over medium-high heat, stirring until the sugar is dissolved. Remove from the heat and let cool to room temperature.

2. Transfer the coconut milk mixture to a medium bowl and refrigerate, tightly covered, for at least 2 hours, until thoroughly chilled, or for up to 2 days.

3. Transfer the chilled coconut milk mixture to a large glass measure and whisk in the pineapple juice, lime juice, and rum (if using). Pour the mixture into an ice-cream maker and freeze according to the manufacturer's instructions. Transfer to a freezer container and freeze for at least 2 hours before serving. (The sorbet is best served on the day it is made.)

4. Spoon the sorbet into serving bowls or glasses to serve.

COCONUT AND MANGO SORBET

SERVES 4 (MAKES A GENEROUS 1 QUART) I love this combination—the coconut and mango together are better than the sum of their parts. If you like, garnish the sorbet with Toasted Coconut Sugar (page 135) stirred together with chopped honey-roasted peanuts. Or perch a Chocolate Coconut Bar (page 137) on the side of each bowl.

¾ CUP WATER

¾ CUP SUGAR

LARGE PINCH OF SALT

2 CUPS FRESH OR WELL-STIRRED CANNED UNSWEETENED COCONUT MILK

1 ½ CUPS SWEETENED MANGO PUREE (SEE PAGE 20)

¼ CUP FRESH LIME JUICE

1. Bring the water, sugar, and salt to a boil in a small saucepan over medium-high heat, stirring until the sugar is dissolved. Reduce the heat and simmer for 3 minutes.

2. Pour the sugar syrup into a large glass measure or a bowl. Whisk in the coconut milk, mango puree, and lime juice until well combined. Refrigerate, tightly covered, for at least 4 hours, until thoroughly chilled, or for up to 2 days.

3. Pour the mixture into an ice-cream maker and freeze according to the manufacturer's instructions. Transfer to a freezer container and freeze for at least 2 hours before serving. (The sorbet is best served on the day it is made.)

4. Spoon the sorbet into serving bowls or glasses, to serve.

COCONUT AND LYCHEE SORBET

**SERVES 4 TO 6
(MAKES 5 CUPS)**

I adore lychee juice, which tastes very much like the fresh fruit. You can buy aseptic packages of the juice in Asian markets, and I've seen them in many supermarkets. This sorbet is not only delicious, it's fun.

½ CUP WATER

½ CUP SUGAR

PINCH OF SALT

2 ½ CUPS CHILLED FRESH OR WELL-STIRRED CANNED UNSWEETENED COCONUT MILK

1 ¾ CUPS CHILLED LYCHEE JUICE

2 TEASPOONS FRESH LIME JUICE

1. Bring the water, sugar, and salt to a boil in a small saucepan over medium-high heat, stirring until the sugar is dissolved. Reduce the heat and simmer for 3 minutes. Remove from the heat and cool to room temperature.

2. Transfer the sugar syrup to a small bowl and refrigerate, tightly covered, for at least 1 hour, until thoroughly chilled, or for up to 2 days.

3. Whisk together the coconut milk and lychee juice in a large glass measure or bowl. Whisk in the chilled syrup and lime juice. Pour the mixture into an ice-cream maker and freeze according to the manufacturer's instructions. Transfer to a freezer container and freeze for at least 2 hours before serving. (The sorbet is best served on the day it is made.)

4. Spoon the sorbet into serving bowls or glasses to serve.

COCONUT AND LEMONGRASS GRANITA

**SERVES 4 TO 6
(MAKES ABOUT
5 CUPS)**

This is elegant served in beautiful stemmed glasses. If you want to doll it up, add a tiny garnish of mint leaves and a scattering of blueberries, finely diced mango tossed with lime, or a sprinkle of toasted fresh coconut ribbons (see page 10) to each serving.

---

2 CUPS WATER

½ CUP SUGAR

1 STALK LEMONGRASS, TRIMMED AND THINLY SLICED

PINCH OF SALT

ONE 13½- OR 14-OUNCE CAN UNSWEET-ENED COCONUT MILK, CHILLED

1. Bring the water, sugar, lemongrass, and salt to a full boil in a medium saucepan over medium-high heat, stirring until the sugar is dissolved. Remove the pan from the heat, cover, and let steep for 15 minutes.

2. Pour the lemongrass mixture through a fine-mesh strainer set over a medium glass measure, pressing hard on the solids to extract as much liquid as possible. Let cool to room temperature, then refrigerate, tightly covered, for at least 2 hours, until thoroughly chilled, or for up to 2 days.

3. Put an 8-inch square baking pan in the freezer to chill.

4. Whisk together the chilled syrup and coconut milk in a large glass measure. Pour the mixture into the cold baking pan. Cover with aluminum foil and freeze for 1 hour, or until ice crystals form around the edges. Stir the mixture well with a fork to incorporate the ice and break up any chunks. Continue to freeze, stirring every 30 minutes, for 3 hours, or until the granita has become granular but is still slightly slushy. The granita can be served now, or it can be frozen for up to 4 hours; stir once or twice to break up any large chunks of ice.

5. Serve the granita in glasses or bowls.

COCONUT AND FRESH GINGER ICE CREAM

SERVES 6 TO 8
(MAKES 1½ QUARTS)

The zing of the fresh ginger really enhances the flavor of the coconut. Beating the egg yolks and sugar with an electric mixer makes for an ice cream with a fantastic texture. It's almost chewy, and it's very creamy. I love this topped with a bit of Coconut-Caramel Popcorn (page 139).

2 CUPS FRESH OR WELL-STIRRED CANNED UNSWEETENED COCONUT MILK

1 CUP SHREDDED UNSWEETENED DRIED COCONUT, TOASTED (SEE PAGE 10)

2 CUPS HEAVY (WHIPPING) CREAM

2 ½ TABLESPOONS MINCED FRESH GINGER

¼ TEASPOON SALT

8 LARGE EGG YOLKS

¾ CUP SUGAR

1. Bring the coconut milk, toasted coconut, cream, ginger, and salt to a full boil in a large heavy saucepan over medium-high heat. Remove the pan from the heat, cover, and let steep for 25 minutes.

2. Pour the cream mixture through a fine-mesh strainer set over a medium glass measure, pressing hard on the solids to extract as much liquid as possible. Rinse and dry the saucepan.

3. Beat the egg yolks and sugar with an electric mixer on medium-high speed in a large deep bowl until very thick and pale and the volume has increased at least three times. Reduce the speed to low and slowly add the cream mixture. Return the mixture to the saucepan and cook over medium-low heat, whisking frequently, for 8 to 10 minutes, until the custard has thickened and coats the back of a spoon. Do not let the custard boil or scorch; if tiny bubbles appear around the edges, remove the pan from the heat for a few minutes to cool the custard, continuing to whisk.

4. Immediately pour the custard through a fine-mesh strainer set over a large glass measure or bowl. Let cool to room temperature, whisking occasionally. Refrigerate, tightly covered, for at least 6 hours, until thoroughly chilled, or for up to 2 days.

5. Pour the mixture into an ice-cream maker and freeze according to the manufacturer's instructions.

6. Transfer to a freezer container and freeze for at least 2 hours before serving.

7. Spoon the ice cream into serving bowls or glasses to serve.

TOASTED COCONUT ICE CREAM

SERVES 4 TO 6
(MAKES 5 CUPS)

Serve this ice cream with a drizzle of Coconut Caramel Sauce (page 131) or Chocolate Coconut Sauce (page 132).

2 CUPS FRESH OR WELL-STIRRED CANNED UNSWEETENED COCONUT MILK

1½ CUPS SHREDDED UNSWEETENED DRIED COCONUT, TOASTED (SEE PAGE 10)

1½ CUPS HEAVY (WHIPPING) CREAM

PINCH OF SALT

8 LARGE EGG YOLKS

½ CUP SHAVED PALM SUGAR OR PACKED LIGHT BROWN SUGAR

1. Bring the coconut milk, toasted coconut, cream, and salt to a full boil in a large heavy saucepan over medium-high heat. Remove the pan from the heat, cover, and let steep for 25 minutes.

2. Pour the cream mixture through a fine-mesh strainer set over a medium glass measure, pressing hard on the solids to extract as much liquid as possible.

3. Beat the egg yolks and sugar with an electric mixer on medium-high speed in a large deep bowl until very thick and pale and the volume has increased at least three times. Reduce the speed to low and slowly add the cream mixture. Return the mixture to the saucepan and cook over medium-low heat, whisking constantly, for 8 to 10 minutes, until the custard has thickened and coats the back of a spoon. Do not let the custard boil or scorch; if tiny bubbles appear around the edges, remove the pan from the heat for a few minutes to cool the custard, continuing to whisk.

4. Immediately pour the custard through a fine-mesh strainer set over a large glass measure or bowl. Let cool to room temperature, whisking occasionally. Refrigerate, tightly covered, for at least 5 hours, until thoroughly chilled, or for up to 2 days.

5. Pour the mixture into an ice-cream maker and freeze according to the manufacturer's instructions.

6. Transfer to a freezer container and freeze for at least 2 hours before serving.

7. Spoon the ice cream into serving bowls or glasses to serve.

TOASTED SNOWBALLS WITH COCONUT CHOCOLATE SAUCE

SERVES 4

Of course you can't toast snowballs, but these do have a nice toasty flavor. You can play around with them—coat some in Toasted Coconut Sugar (page 135) or crushed Coconut Praline (page 138), or make many tiny ones.

3 CUPS TOASTED COCONUT ICE CREAM (PAGE 124) OR YOUR FAVORITE ICE CREAM, SLIGHTLY SOFTENED

1 CUP SWEETENED FLAKED COCONUT, TOASTED (SEE PAGE 10)

1 CUP COCONUT CHOCOLATE SAUCE (PAGE 132)

1. Line a large plate with wax paper and chill in the freezer for 10 minutes.

2. Working quickly, scoop 12 balls of ice cream, using ¼ cup for each snowball, and transfer to the wax-paper-lined plate. Freeze for 30 minutes, or until firm.

3. Put the coconut on a plate. Roll the ice-cream balls in the coconut to coat completely and return to the wax-paper-lined plate. Cover and freeze for at least 1 hour, or for up to 2 days.

4. Pour ¼ cup of the chocolate sauce into the center of each of 4 serving plates. Top each with 3 snow-balls, and serve immediately.

GINGER BEER ICE CREAM FLOAT

SERVES 1

This is also fantastic made with sorbet. From this book, choose the Piña Colada Sorbet (page 117), Coconut and Lychee Sorbet (page 119), or Coconut and Mango Sorbet (page 118).

ONE 12-OUNCE BOTTLE GINGER BEER, EXTRA-DRY GINGER ALE, OR GINGER ALE, CHILLED

1 CUP COCONUT AND FRESH GINGER ICE CREAM (PAGE 122), TOASTED COCONUT ICE CREAM (PAGE 124), OR YOUR FAVORITE ICE CREAM

1. Pour about ¼ cup of the ginger beer into a tall chilled glass, add about ¼ cup of the ice cream, and stir until the ice cream is melted and the mixture is smooth. Slowly pour enough ginger beer down the side of the glass to fill it about half-full. Add the remaining ice cream, and if there is room left in the glass, add more ginger beer.

2. Serve immediately, with a straw, a long-handled spoon, and the bottle of ginger beer, if there is any remaining.

SAUCES, GARNISHES, AND CANDIES

Think of the recipes in this chapter as mix-and-match accessories for coconut and other desserts.

They are a convenient and tasty way to layer coconut flavors and textures in a coconut dessert and to add coconut flavors to those that aren't. There are endless ways to use these sauces. Serve the Coconut Lover's Coconut Custard Sauce (page 130) with another coconut dessert or fresh tropical fruit, like mango. Or drizzle the Coconut Caramel Sauce (page 131) over the Lighter-than-Air Coconut Jelly (page 89), Tropical Eton Mess (page 109), or Matrimony (page 106). The Coconut Chocolate Sauce (page 132) is grand when you want to add both coconut and chocolate flavor. The Luscious Coconut and Mango Curd (page 134) is good on just about everything, including your morning toast. Toasted Coconut Syrup (page 135) makes a great quick drizzle over desserts, and Coconut Dulce de Leche (page 132) is terrific as a dip for fresh fruit or as a spread between cake layers. The Coconut Whipped Cream (page 140) is simple to make when you're craving coconut.

The garnishes and candies are practically interchangeable. All have a deep coconut flavor, look great, and, above all, are fun. Coconut-Caramel Popcorn (page 139) makes a whimsical garnish, equally good with a serious sophisticated dessert like the Bittersweet Chocolate and Coconut Tart (page 61) or something down-home like the Bananas Foster Shortcake with Coconut Biscuits (page 102). Use Candied Coconut (page 141), Coconut Praline (page 138), or Toasted Coconut Sugar (page 135) on the whole lot—they are beautiful and really highlight the flavor and the look of coconut. Perch a Chocolate Coconut Bar (page 137), which is like a Mounds bar made with high-quality chocolate, or a Marshmallow Lamington (page 140) on the side of a coconut dessert or your after-dinner coffee cup. And the Caramelized Pineapple (page 141) is the perfect accessory to many coconut desserts.

COCONUT LOVER'S
COCONUT CUSTARD SAUCE

Although vanilla belongs in most custard sauces, in this version (pictured on page 133, center), the vanilla would fight a bit with the coconut. But coconut rum enhances the coconut flavor, so for me that's a better choice. You could add a pandan leaf (see page 20) to the coconut steeping liquid for an aromatic tropical flavor. Serve the sauce with the Coconut, Almond, and Lime Macaroon Cake (page 30).

MAKES A SCANT 3 CUPS

1 ½ CUPS HALF-AND-HALF

¾ CUP SHREDDED UNSWEETENED
DRIED COCONUT, TOASTED (SEE PAGE 10)

½ CUP FRESH OR WELL-STIRRED CANNED
UNSWEETENED COCONUT MILK

6 LARGE EGG YOLKS

½ CUP SUGAR

PINCH OF SALT

1 TO 2 TABLESPOONS COCONUT RUM,
PREFERABLY MALIBU (OPTIONAL)

1. Bring the half-and half, toasted coconut, and coconut milk to a full boil in a medium heavy saucepan over medium-high heat, stirring occasionally. Remove the pan from the heat, cover, and let steep for 25 minutes.

2. Pour the half-and-half mixture through a fine-mesh strainer set over a medium glass measure, pressing hard on the solids to extract as much liquid as possible. Rinse and dry the saucepan.

3. Whisk together the egg yolks, sugar, and salt in a medium bowl. Slowly pour in the half-and-half mixture, whisking constantly. Return to the saucepan and cook, whisking constantly, over medium-low heat until the custard has thickened and coats the back of a spoon; if you draw your finger across it, it should leave a track. Do not let the sauce boil or scorch; if tiny bubbles appear around the edges, remove the pan from the heat for a few minutes to cool the custard, continuing to whisk.

4. Whisk in the coconut rum (if using). Pour the custard through a fine-mesh strainer set over a medium glass measure or bowl. Use immediately, or let cool to room temperature, whisking occasionlly to keep a skin from forming, and refrigerate, tightly covered, for at least 3 hours to serve chilled, or for up to 4 days. Serve chilled, or reheat gently to serve warm.

COCONUT CARAMEL SAUCE

I love caramel sauce (pictured on page 133, right). This one not only has the lovely bitter and sweet of the caramel itself, the smoothness of cream and butter, and the lush tropical coconut, it also has the vigor of fresh lime and ginger. If you'd like to intensify the coconut flavor, you can add ¼ teaspoon or so of pure coconut extract after the sauce has cooled.

MAKES 2 CUPS

1 CUP HEAVY (WHIPPING) CREAM

¾ CUP SHREDDED UNSWEETENED DRIED COCONUT, TOASTED (SEE PAGE 10)

1 TABLESPOON FINELY CHOPPED FRESH GINGER

1 TEASPOON FINELY GRATED LIME ZEST

¼ CUP (½ STICK) UNSALTED BUTTER, AT ROOM TEMPERATURE

2 CUPS SUGAR

½ CUP WATER

PINCH OF SALT

1 TO 3 TABLESPOONS COCONUT RUM, PREFERABLY MALIBU (OPTIONAL)

1. Bring the cream, toasted coconut, ginger, and lime zest to a full boil in a medium heavy saucepan over medium-high heat. Remove the pan from the heat, cover, and let steep for 25 minutes.

2. Pour the cream mixture through a fine-mesh strainer set over a medium glass measure, pressing hard on the solids to extract as much liquid as possible. Whisk in the butter.

3. Heat the sugar, water, and salt in a large heavy saucepan over medium heat, stirring, until the sugar is dissolved. Increase the heat to high and bring the mixture to a boil, washing down the sides of the pan with a wet pastry brush if you see any sugar crystals. Boil, without stirring, swirling the pan toward the end to even out the color, until the caramel is a dark amber. Immediately remove the saucepan from the heat. Let stand for about 1 minute, or until most of the bubbles have subsided.

4. Being careful to avoid spatters, stir the cream mixture into the caramel, about 2 tablespoons at a time. Return the pan to low heat and cook, whisking, until well combined and smooth. Whisk in the coconut rum (if using). Use immediately, or let cool to room temperature and refrigerate, tightly covered, for up to 2 months. Serve chilled, or gently reheat the sauce before serving, adding a little water or cream if necessary to thin it slightly.

COCONUT CHOCOLATE SAUCE

Chocolate is very intense (isn't that why we love it?) and can easily overwhelm coconut. You have to balance the flavors, and in this instance, the sauce (pictured on facing page, left) needs either coconut rum or coconut extract to give the flaked coconut the boost it needs to stand up to the chocolate.

MAKES 1 CUP

1 CUP HEAVY (WHIPPING) CREAM

½ CUP SWEETENED FLAKED COCONUT, TOASTED (SEE PAGE 10) IF DESIRED

PINCH OF SALT

4 OUNCES BITTERSWEET OR SEMISWEET CHOCOLATE, FINELY CHOPPED

1 TABLESPOON COCONUT RUM, PREFERABLY MALIBU (OPTIONAL), OR ¼ TEASPOON PURE COCONUT EXTRACT

1. Bring the cream, coconut, and salt to a full boil in a medium heavy saucepan over medium heat. Remove from the heat, cover, and let steep for 25 minutes.

2. Pour the cream mixture through a fine-mesh strainer set over a medium glass measure, pressing hard on the solids to extract as much liquid as possible.

3. Return the cream mixture to the saucepan, set over low heat, add the chocolate, and cook, whisking constantly, for about 2 minutes, until melted and smooth. Whisk in the rum (if using). Use immediately, or refrigerate, tightly covered, for up to 1 week. Reheat gently.

COCONUT DULCE DE LECHE

I was inspired to make this creamy confection by a recipe in *Bon Appétit* magazine. You can use it as a dipping sauce, as a filling for cakes, or to make sandwich cookies.

MAKES 1 ¼ CUPS

TWO 13 ½- OR 14-OUNCE CANS UNSWEETENED COCONUT MILK

½ CUP SHREDDED UNSWEETENED DRIED COCONUT, TOASTED (SEE PAGE 10)

1 CUP SHAVED PALM SUGAR OR PACKED LIGHT BROWN SUGAR

½ TEASPOON SALT

1. Combine the coconut milk, toasted coconut, sugar, and salt in a large deep heavy saucepan and cook over medium heat, whisking occasionally, until the sugar is dissolved. Bring to a boil over medium-high heat, then reduce the heat slightly and cook at a rolling boil, whisking frequently and being careful the mixture does not boil over, for about 30 minutes, until reduced by about half.

2. Pour through a fine-mesh strainer set over a medium glass measure, pressing hard on the solids to extract as much liquid as possible. Let cool to room temperature. The dulce de leche can be refrigerated, tightly covered, for up to 1 month. This is best served at room temperature.

LUSCIOUS COCONUT AND MANGO CURD

Look for Ratnā or Swad brand canned sweetened mango puree in Asian markets. The flavor of mango puree is better than that of many fresh mangoes, and because these brands are made with luscious Indian mangoes, the puree has no fibers and is perfectly smooth. You could substitute a couple of tablespoons of palm sugar or brown sugar for some of the granulated sugar in the recipe and the curd will taste great because of the caramel undertone—but if you use too much, it will change the color from a vibrant orange to a brownish orange.

MAKES 1½ CUPS

½ CUP (1 STICK) UNSALTED BUTTER

⅓ CUP SWEETENED FLAKED COCONUT

¾ CUP CANNED SWEETENED MANGO PUREE

½ CUP SUGAR

LARGE PINCH OF SALT

6 LARGE EGG YOLKS

3 TABLESPOONS FRESH LIME JUICE

1. Melt the butter in a large heavy saucepan over medium heat. Add the coconut and cook, stirring occasionally, for 4 to 5 minutes, until the coconut is lightly toasted.

2. Remove the pan from the heat and whisk in the mango puree, sugar, and salt. Whisk in the egg yolks. Return the saucepan to medium heat and cook, whisking frequently at first and constantly at the end, for 6 to 8 minutes, until thickened. Immediately pour the curd through a fine-mesh strainer set over a medium glass measure or bowl, pressing hard on the solids to extract as much liquid as possible. Cool to room temperature, whisking occasionally; the curd will continue to thicken as it cools.

3. Whisk in the lime juice. Refrigerate, covered, for at least 2 hours, until thoroughly chilled and set, or for up to 2 weeks.

TOASTED COCONUT SYRUP

Use this to make a very speedy coconut ice cream soda: Pour about 3 tablespoons of the syrup into a tall glass and stir in about ¼ cup of your favorite ice cream or sorbet until well combined. Then pour seltzer into the glass to fill it about half-full, add about ¾ cup more ice cream, and top with whipped cream and a sprinkle of toasted coconut.

MAKES 1 CUP

1 ½ CUPS WATER

1 CUP SWEETENED FLAKED COCONUT, TOASTED (SEE PAGE 10)

3 TABLESPOONS LIGHT CORN SYRUP

PINCH OF SALT

A SQUEEZE OF FRESH LIME JUICE

1. Bring the water, toasted coconut, corn syrup, and salt just to a boil in a medium saucepan over medium-high heat. Reduce the heat and cook at a low boil for 15 minutes, until slightly thickened. Remove the pan from the heat and stir in the lime juice.

2. Pour the syrup through a fine-mesh strainer set over a medium glass measure, pressing hard on the solids to extract as much liquid as possible. Let cool to room temperature, then transfer to a glass jar and refrigerate for about 1 hour, or until thoroughly chilled, or for up to 1 month. Shake vigorously before serving.

TOASTED COCONUT SUGAR

Coconut lovers will find infinite uses for this coconut brown sugar. It's wonderful in your nightly hot milk or hot chocolate. Add it to smoothies, baked goods, or frostings, or use it to make coconut-cinnamon toast. Sprinkle it over sugar cookies, fruits, or cold or hot cereal. Roll chocolate truffles in it or use it to top the whipped cream on a hot fudge sundae, or to garnish just about anything sweet. I also like to stir together a cup of the coconut sugar with about half as much finely chopped honey-roasted almonds or candied pecans to use as a garnish. Large shreds of coconut have more flavor, and this also looks nicer if you use a large shred.

MAKES 4 CUPS

3 CUPS SHREDDED UNSWEETENED DRIED COCONUT (SEE HEADNOTE)

1 CUP PACKED LIGHT BROWN SUGAR

1. Preheat the oven to 300°F.

2. Using a fork, combine the coconut and sugar in a medium bowl, breaking up any lumps of sugar or clumps of coconut. Spread on a large heavy baking sheet and toast in the oven, stirring three times, for about 30 minutes, until golden brown and dry. Cool to room temperature on the pan on a wire rack.

3. Transfer the coconut sugar to an airtight container. Store at room temperature for up to 3 months or more.

CHOCOLATE COCONUT BARS

This recipe (pictured on facing page, bottom) is adapted from a version in *Gourmet* magazine developed by test kitchen director Ruth Cousineau. Add half a cup or so of chopped pistachios or darkly toasted almonds to the coconut mixture, if you want.

MAKES 16 BARS

½ CUP SHREDDED UNSWEETENED DRIED COCONUT, TOASTED (SEE PAGE 10)

1 CUP SWEETENED FLAKED COCONUT

⅓ CUP SWEETENED CONDENSED MILK

¼ TEASPOON PURE VANILLA EXTRACT

PINCH OF SALT

4 OUNCES BITTERSWEET OR SEMISWEET CHOCOLATE, FINELY CHOPPED

1. Line an 8-inch square baking pan with wax paper, leaving a 2-inch overhang on two opposite sides. Stir together the toasted coconut, sweetened coconut, condensed milk, vanilla, and salt with a rubber spatula in a medium bowl. Press the mixture into the pan, making an even layer. Chill for at least 15 minutes, or until firm and set. (The coconut layer can be refrigerated, tightly covered, for up to 2 days.)

2. Melt the chocolate in a heatproof bowl set over a saucepan of about 1½ inches of barely simmering water, whisking until smooth. Pour the chocolate over the coconut layer and spread with a small offset spatula to coat evenly. Chill for about 15 minutes, until firm and set.

3. Using the wax paper "handles," lift the candy onto a work surface. Cut it in half with a sharp knife. Sandwich the halves together, coconut-side in, if you like. Discard the wax paper. Cut the candy lengthwise into 4 strips, then cut each strip crosswise into 4 strips. The bars can be refrigerated, tightly covered, for up to 2 weeks.

COCONUT PRALINE

Praline is one of the world's great sweets, and coconut praline (pictured on page 136, top) is gorgeous and delicious. Wide-cut unsweetened dried coconut is beautiful, and it's even more attractive when it is toasted. You could use shredded coconut here, but you'll be happier with the wide-cut. Break the praline into big shards, coarsely crush it, or process it to a fine powder, depending on what you're using it for. The powder will spoil quickly at room temperature, so store it in the freezer. You could replace half a cup or so of the coconut with bright green, unsalted pistachios to give the praline a great look. The corn syrup helps to prevent crystallization.

MAKES 1 POUND

1 ½ CUPS WIDE-CUT UNSWEETENED DRIED COCONUT, TOASTED (SEE PAGE 10)

1 ½ CUPS SUGAR

⅓ CUP WATER

1 TABLESPOON LIGHT CORN SYRUP

PINCH OF SALT

1. Arrange the coconut close together in a circle that is about 8 inches in diameter on a baking sheet.

2. Heat the sugar, water, corn syrup, and salt in a medium heavy saucepan over medium heat, stirring, until the sugar dissolves. Increase the heat to high and bring the mixture to a boil, washing down the sides of the pan with a wet pastry brush if you see any sugar crystals. Boil, without stirring, swirling the pan toward the end to even out the color, until the caramel is a dark amber. Immediately pour the caramel in a circular motion over the coconut to coat it evenly. If necessary, move the mixture around with a fork to ensure all of the coconut is submerged and coated, but be careful—the fork can get very hot. Let the praline stand for about 15 minutes to cool and harden.

3. For shards, break the praline into large or medium pieces. For coarsely ground praline, break into smaller pieces, put in a self-sealing plastic bag, and crush with a rolling pin into the size you need. For praline powder, pulse small pieces in a food processor until finely ground.

COCONUT-CARAMEL POPCORN

A delightful casual dessert on its own, this also makes a gorgeous and surprising garnish. I especially like it on the Bittersweet Chocolate and Coconut Tart (page 61).

MAKES ABOUT 4 QUARTS

3 ½ QUARTS FRESHLY POPPED POPCORN (ABOUT ½ CUP UNPOPPED)

1 ¼ CUPS PACKED LIGHT BROWN SUGAR

½ CUP (1 STICK) UNSALTED BUTTER, CUT INTO 8 PIECES

¼ CUP LIGHT CORN SYRUP

1 ½ CUPS WIDE-CUT (SEE PAGE 13) OR SHREDDED UNSWEETENED DRIED COCONUT, TOASTED (SEE PAGE 10)

½ CUP COARSELY CHOPPED UNSALTED CASHEWS

½ CUP COARSELY CHOPPED UNSALTED PISTACHIOS OR MACADAMIA NUTS

1 TABLESPOON FINELY CHOPPED CRYSTALLIZED GINGER

½ TEASPOON SALT

½ TEASPOON BAKING SODA

1. Preheat the oven to 200°F.

2. Put the popcorn in a large bowl.

3. Bring the brown sugar, butter, and corn syrup to a boil in a large heavy saucepan over medium heat, stirring until the sugar is dissolved. Boil for 5 minutes. Remove the pan from the heat and stir in the toasted coconut, cashews, pistachios, ginger, salt, and baking soda; the mixture will foam up. Pour over the popcorn and toss until evenly coated. Be careful, the sugar mixture is very hot.

4. Spread the popcorn mixture evenly on two large heavy baking sheets. Bake for 1 hour, stirring 3 times and switching the pans from top to bottom and front to back each time. Let cool completely on the pans.

5. Break the popcorn into large pieces. It can be stored in an airtight container at room temperature for up to 2 weeks.

MARSHMALLOW LAMINGTONS

Lamingtons are an Australian specialty consisting of small squares of sponge cake coated with chocolate and coconut. This is a marshmallow version (pictured on page 136, middle). "Gourmet" marshmallows are widely available in specialty foods stores; use them if you'd like. Serve these with coffee or use as a garnish.

MAKES 30 PIECES

8 OUNCES BITTERSWEET OR SEMISWEET CHOCOLATE, CHOPPED

1 TABLESPOON FLAVORLESS VEGETABLE OIL

1 CUP SHREDDED UNSWEETENED DRIED COCONUT, TOASTED (SEE PAGE 10) IF DESIRED

30 MARSHMALLOWS

1. Melt the chocolate with the oil in a heat-proof bowl set over a saucepan of about 1½ inches of barely simmering water, whisking until smooth. Remove the bowl from the heat.

2. Spread the coconut on a sheet of wax paper. Hold each marshmallow with a toothpick and coat with chocolate, shaking off the excess, then roll in the coconut, shaking off the excess, and transfer to a wire rack. (If the chocolate gets too thick for dipping, return the bowl to the saucepan for a minute or two.) Let the marshmallows stand for 30 minutes, or until the chocolate is set.

COCONUT WHIPPED CREAM

This coconutty whipped cream is especially impressive with cakes and pies. You can add a tablespoon or two of coconut rum in addition to or instead of the coconut extract.

MAKES ABOUT 2 CUPS

1 CUP HEAVY (WHIPPING) CREAM

2 TABLESPOONS CONFECTIONERS' SUGAR

½ TEASPOON PURE COCONUT EXTRACT (SEE PAGE 17)

Beat the cream with an electric mixer on medium-high speed in a large deep bowl just until the cream holds soft peaks when the beaters are lifted. Beat in the sugar and coconut extract. The whipped cream can be made up to 4 hours ahead and refrigerated tightly covered.

CANDIED COCONUT

This is my favorite coconut garnish and I use it with just about anything. It is beautiful, tastes great, and has splendid texture. Feel free to double the recipe; it keeps very well.

MAKES ABOUT 2 ¾ CUPS

2 TABLESPOONS WATER

2 TABLESPOONS GRANULATED SUGAR

PINCH OF SALT

2 CUPS WIDE-CUT UNSWEETENED DRIED COCONUT (SEE PAGE 13)

2 TABLESPOONS TURBINADO SUGAR (SEE COOK'S NOTE, PAGE 32)

1. Preheat the oven to 400°F. Line a large heavy baking sheet with a silicone baking mat.

2. Bring the water, granulated sugar, and salt to a boil in a small saucepan over medium heat, stirring until the sugar is dissolved. Transfer the syrup to a medium bowl, stir in the coconut, and toss until evenly coated. Sprinkle with the turbinado sugar and toss until evenly coated.

3. Spread the coconut on the baking sheet and bake, stirring with a wide metal spatula and turning the pan around halfway through, for about 10 minutes, until golden brown. Let cool completely on the pan on a wire rack.

4. Break the coconut into pieces. Store in an airtight container for up to 1 month.

CARAMELIZED PINEAPPLE

Try this with the Coconut Crème Brûlée Tart (page 55), either of the coconut jellies (pages 89 and 92), or the Piña Colada Sorbet (page 117). You might add a couple of tablespoons of coconut rum or diced firm ripe mango along with the pineapple.

MAKES ABOUT 2 CUPS

⅔ CUP SUGAR

¼ CUP WATER

PINCH OF SALT

3 CUPS ½-INCH-DICE FRESH PINEAPPLE

3 TABLESPOONS FRESH LIME JUICE, OR TO TASTE

1. Heat the sugar, water, and salt in a medium heavy saucepan over medium heat, stirring, until the sugar is dissolved. Increase the heat to high and bring the mixture to a boil, washing down the sides of the pan with a wet pastry brush if you see any sugar crystals. Boil, without stirring, swirling the pan toward the end to even out the color, until the caramel is a medium amber. Immediately remove the saucepan from the heat.

2. Being careful to avoid spatters, gradually stir in the pineapple and lime juice. Return the pan to low heat and cook, stirring gently, until well combined and any lumps of caramel are dissolved. Taste and add more lime juice, if desired. Use immediately, or let cool and refrigerate, tightly covered, for up to 2 days. Gently reheat the pineapple before serving, if desired.

INDEX

TABLE OF EQUIVALENTS

The exact equivalents in the following tables have been rounded for convenience.

LIQUID/DRY MEASUREMENTS		LENGTHS		OVEN TEMPERATURE		
U.S.	METRIC	U.S.	METRIC	FAHRENHEIT	CELSIUS	GAS
¼ teaspoon	1.25 milliliters	⅛ inch	3 millimeters	250	120	½
½ teaspoon	2.5 milliliters	¼ inch	6 millimeters	275	140	1
1 teaspoon	5 milliliters	½ inch	12 millimeters	300	150	2
1 tablespoon (3 teaspoons)	15 milliliters	1 inch	2.5 centimeters	325	160	3
1 fluid ounce (2 tablespoons)	30 milliliters			350	180	4
¼ cup	60 milliliters			375	190	5
⅓ cup	80 milliliters			400	200	6
½ cup	120 milliliters			425	220	7
1 cup	240 milliliters			450	230	8
1 pint (2 cups)	480 milliliters			475	240	9
1 quart (4 cups, 32 ounces)	960 milliliters			500	260	10
1 gallon (4 quarts)	3.84 liters					
1 ounce (by weight)	28 grams					
1 pound	448 grams					
2.2 pounds	1 kilogram